MATTERS OF LIFE AND DEATH

-

Essays in Budô

Peter Barus

MATTERS OF LIFE AND DEATH

To my Sensei,

Mr. F. J. Lovret

ACKNOWLEDGMENTS

If there is anything polished and useful in me, emerging from the forge of Budô, it is as much the creation of Mr. A. H. Rajguru as a sword is the creation of the smith.

Some who "pulled me to my feet" over the years, and continue without reserve: William Knight, Adam Schutz, Savvas Savopoulos, Joseph Simms, Richard Gilbert, Andrew Stevenson, Michael Kelly, Randy Mamiaro, Steve Weiss, Nicholas Busan, Rick Ritacco, William Maren, Robert Schmitt, Lynn Reafsnyder, Joseph McVey, Edward Collins, Robert Lange, Philp Scudieri, Michael Graves, James Herndon.

Fred Tart, Jerry Ostrowski, Regi Brisbane and Josh Freeman, who lighted the way.

For other editorial and philosophical guidance: Kristina Strom, Rebecca Sadlon.

Friends and relations: John McKendry, Ted Nelson, Peter Colin, Warren Phinney, Margaret Rawson, Jim Richardson, Mary Sage Shakespeare, Anne & George Saxton, Barbara Simonds, Anne & David Seeley, David Barus. My parents, Carl Barus, Barbara Barus Marshall, James Marshall, my wife Lisë Hattoon Barus, son Christopher, brothers William and Maxwell.

Regi Brisbane was my colleague and my friend for over twenty years. "In love and cooking, reckless abandon."

We live, to the extent we do, in the generous awareness of others. The author humbly thanks you for the life you have given him.

Any errors are mine alone.

It is for those yet to be that we write it all down.

ESSAYS IN BUDÔ

CONTENTS

MATTERS OF LIFE AND DEATH

1 KATA

Our sword points an inch apart, there is the stillness of a mantis about to strike. Which of us is prey and which predator? The slightest disturbance will set us off. The Japanese word is *suki*, an opportunity, a distraction. A blink. A thought. We stand unblinking, unthinking, breathing in unison, empty. Swords forged in another age utterly motionless. Far above, autumn wind sighs in the branches.

A leaf falls; the arc of my blade is through the center of his head – but he is not there, he is back about ten feet, blade held low, pointing at my right eye. I go after him – only to arch back painfully, his point at my throat, sweeping up past my chin, missing my wrists by next to nothing. The stroke carries him up on his toes, his arms stretched high above his head. I unbend like a drawn bow, cutting down furiously – but he has spun to the left in midair, and I feel the silky sensation of a polished edge on the back of my neck.

He steps back, sword low, as I turn, matching his stance. Like cats we move to the line again, an inch between our blades.

Then, he attacks.

In the beginning, a *kumitachi* seems to be a precisely choreographed re-enactment of a battle. For years we practice each tiny detail of each movement, only much later distinguishing attack, evasion and counter. Eventually, with correct practice, principles emerge, not just tactics, but strategies, a world view embedded in this conversation-of-action. And then, one day, there is no difference between performance and the real thing. It is exactly as fast, and as deadly. And, there is no fear, no violence, no thought.

No me.

MATTERS OF LIFE AND DEATH

2 INTRODUCTION

I began this project in about 1994, after a decade of training in an old Japanese sword tradition. I thought I was writing about martial arts.

At the outset of the reader's journey through this Mulligan stew of recollections, discoveries and reflections it is only fair to state clearly that this is not a scholarly treatise on Japanese swordsmanship or a sensational, purportedly definitive book on the mysteries of martial arts. It is a personal account of practice in an art. It will include some things that may not be accessible to scholars, and also neglect points that would seem basic. In the attempt to put experience into words, there is always a question of whether the words refer to some actuality or to some imagined event. Even recounting what has happened, the account is imaginary. This is simply a fact of neurology. I hope to point to something, as one points to the moon, after which the pointing is of no particular importance.

We speak about attention as though we can direct it in accordance with the right priorities, waste it or spend it wisely, have it stolen or manipulated, let it wander or keep it on a short leash. On the other hand, infants do not thrive without attention from others. Like the heart, it is central to life, but works automatically; like breathing, we have some say in the matter of its operation. It is susceptible to malfunctions and outside interference. We pay attention, get too much attention or not enough, and so on. We may be both its master and its slave.

In the school rooms of my childhood, when it came to my attention, it had wandered, was too focused, not focused enough, distracted, too short. I didn't pay enough to what was thought important. Since I was frequently taken to task for this, I might have assumed I could or should learn to manage whatever it was. But when called on the carpet for not paying attention, outwardly I expressed contrition to lighten punishment; inwardly I had no idea except that somehow I was expected to be different in some way. In such moments of discomfort I and my classmates designed our future lives. If this is not so for all of us, we are no less the inhabitants of a world where this kind of duplicity holds sway by general, unspoken agreement. Everyone pretends to pay attention, but we exploit, and suffer greatly from, the fact that we do not.

The brain shuts out vision when the eye is in motion, omitting tiny intervals of blindness, providing a seamless but ultimately false perception of the visual environment. No doubt a similar function allows the semblance of truly simultaneous multitasking. But no matter how many things we may be able to keep in the air for awhile, the similarity to juggling is obvious when we drop one.

Stage magicians know that attention is very easily captured and misdirected; it is the raw material of the illusionist's art. Pickpockets and card sharps use similar, subtle techniques. Our brains are suggestible and easily blinded to the obvious. But this is the tip of a very large iceberg.

Beginning with one Eddie Bernays, nephew of Freud, the Public Relations industry was born. Women were induced to smoke tobacco; when the package color clashed with popular fashions, Bernays is credited with changing, not the tobacco packaging, but women's fashions of the time. With the advent of computer communications technologies this new hybrid art-science has made the aggregated attention of large numbers of people a resource to be packaged and bought and sold like any other commodity.

Mass attention may well be the dominant medium of exchange – and this certainly includes political power – in the modern world, like bronze in the Bronze Age. Bernays lived for over one hundred years, and continued to have an almost mystical public influence until his death in the nineteen sixties. Next to him, Machiavelli was a mere dilettante.

It is important to keep in mind that we are dealing primarily with attention, and that information is a component of this. Developments in mass-media and information management have led to refinements in attention management technologies, at first in selling products. It has become an efficient means of social control. There is a countervailing black market, as it were, in opposition, and while it is possible that the methods predated the madness, the madness is with us for better or worse.

Ancient texts from feudal societies have become quite popular in these times, and if feudalism is not in ascendancy today, it is an appropriate metaphor. Taken as a whole, much of humanity now lives in an economic context very similar to that of the warring city-states of bygone eras.

It may be that this describes today's version of an eternal human condition. The startling relevance of writings from centuries past (e.g., "The Art Of War" and "Book Of Five Rings") seems to point to this. On the other hand, old ways may be obsolete, for creatures that evolved in small communities competing for resources. Given a world of seven billion souls, what once sustained us may now be poison. We are simply running out of space. The swing back to equilibrium, when it comes, will be felt in proportion to the tensions among the forces in play.

Everyone is aware of our situation to some degree of comprehension. Responses range from complacent denial to anger to bargaining to acceptance of our fate – the same list of reactions we have to death – but however we see our future, almost all of us experience it in terms of what has happened before. This colors and shapes life, and hence our responses or reactions. The idea that there is some truth or knowledge just beyond our grasp is a tantalizing one, to our utilitarian way of thinking. Much more rare is the notion that nothing is wrong, and that this moment, whatever seems to be going on, is "all that is the case."

For individuals, then, the salient question might be whether you are, or can be, responsible for your own attention – packaged and traded on the markets as it seems now to be.

3 REAL AND/OR APPARENT

When I was four years old they said I was seeing double. They were guessing. I should have been seeing double, since my eyeballs were obviously aimed in two different directions; but the brain, the wonderful clump of neurons behind them, shut the left one off. To me the world was flat, but singular.

After the surgery I was blind for a couple of weeks. Giant invisible toys seemed to be everywhere I turned. Then the bandages came off, and I peered into a device, and they said to watch and say when the tiger flipped over. I could not see a tiger. Possibly it was being shown to only one eye at a time. The operation was successful, in that I no longer looked like a severely cross-eyed toddler. But the world remained as two-dimensional as Flatland.

I compensated with perspective. The art teacher was impressed with my grasp of vanishing points and logarithmically spaced telephone poles and parallel railroad tracks that meet. But the gym coach was not; baseballs coming right at me in left field suddenly reversed direction, straight down into the catcher's mitt. A few years later they said I couldn't see well. I insisted that I could count every leaf on the tree in my front yard. Then the glasses arrived, and I could See. It was like putting my head in a magic portal to another dimension. But what else was apparent, but not real, in my world? It was not the first time everything I knew turned out to be out of focus.

Although the experts assured me that my brain would not learn to see depth after the age of nine, this did happen eventually. I was thirty, and had just climbed up a very high cliff, and then a very tall tree, and strapped myself to a pully on a steel cable stretched across a lake. I stepped off into thin air. Zip! I was flying! Suddenly the world was deep and wide!

For much of my life I thought of myself as being against violence. The question was framed in religious, moral terms. My parents and uncles and aunts had all been to war, a World War. The overwhelming consensus was that it was futile and pointless and evil, although We Won, and it was Over. In the nineteen-fifties, it was not a subject for polite conversation. Veterans would change the subject if it came up. I grew up proud of my peaceful Nation, believing war would never come again, because we were such a strong people, and a good people, a people that knew right from wrong. A whole country that was against war ever happening again!

I believed that violence was part of a world of rewards and punishments, as every child must. Like most of my peers, I understood that certain behaviors would intensify or diminish this often painful contrast. Since I was apparently successful at navigating these waters to satisfy basic needs, I believed this was an interactive system, a kind of agreement with the world outside myself. Violence was held safely at bay by good behavior (or the appearance of same), grown-ups, policemen and soldiers, and the faithful family dog. As children we avoided cracks in the sidewalks, mindful of our mother's fragile vertebrae; my approach in the matter of violence was equally absurd and childish. I thought if criminals could just be sat down and talked to, they would see the light.

For years I kept insisting that if I held up my end of the bargain, life would respond in kind. It was not until nearly middle age that my illusions about violence were shattered. Looking back the pattern is obvious. This awakening was only the last in a series of confrontations that became more insistent and undeniable until even I could see what was so.

In early childhood nightmares, a mysterious force dragged me toward the dark cellar doorway, down the stairs into the dark, from which I would emerge into bright lights and green-swathed faces and a voice that said: "Hmmmmm." My pre-verbal self could not know that this was merely my birth in familiar symbols, the memory of emerging among a group of obstetricians awaiting my first breath. I awoke in terror, disoriented and screaming.

At the age of three I ran joyfully in a grassy, sunny field, tumbling over and over. Coming to rest on my back, I saw faces above me. But this time they were Big Kids, seven-year-olds! One said: "I'm gonna kill ya!" Living in a world of literal truth, I ran to my father, who merely grunted, barely looking up from his work. Instead of making the obvious inference from my father's indifference, that not everything people say is necessarily so, I concluded in that moment that there would be no help from that quarter; I was on my own.

In later years I walked the mile to school in dread. Groups of other kids devised ingenious new ways to annoy me every day. Nothing satisfied them except my humiliation. Eventually the accident of adolescence made me larger and stronger than most of them, but the ego insists on its version of reality. I clung to the idea that there was some way to negotiate with the world and have it my way.

This was not non-violence, I hasten to say: non-violence recognizes violence, and if necessary, simply chooses death, rather than murder. It is a way of supreme courage and integrity, and I have seen it in action. I have had great teachers in this area, some quite well-known, but I must admit that this way was too steep for me at the time.

Naturally this constrained existence became smaller with each brush against its boundaries until I began to resist. I began to try to find out, a phrase, as the comedian and actor Robin Williams remarked, to conjure with. To find Out.

Mind-altering substances offered possibilities, and for a time provided the illusion of freedom and even power.

Then I ran afoul of some professional criminals. The same old scenario played itself out, more or less. But now I knew beyond any doubt that my death might actually be quite convenient and even entertaining for these people. I had a glimpse of the world as I had never allowed myself to see it. I was aware with an immediacy that stopped my breath, that I would die; and at the same time, that this was utterly trivial. It would matter not at all. In this new world my life was meaningless, and I could lose it by mistake, between one flippant word and the next.

I now saw that my relationship to violence was more like that of a toddler with a loaded gun. I saw exactly how I had made this mess. There had been no accidents, no random coincidences, I saw each and every choice I had made, that had led inexorably to this moment. At each opportunity I had decided something calculated to prop up a fictional character, and now that character had stepped in something that could well be fatal. It all unwound in front of me so clearly, the stupid lie I had tried to put over on the world all those years. Nobody had bought it but me.

Then, with blindingly logical precision, the realization dawned that I must have underestimated the real power at my disposal: if I had made this big a mess of my life, what could I not accomplish? I need no longer sustain the pretense of victimhood. The source of violence was not outside myself. It was myself.

The game was up. All that I had feared proved to be bad memories. Now I had some work to do. I was the proverbial bull in a china shop. It was not for myself that I should fear, but for people around this walking powder-keg of delusions. It was like waking up in a moving vehicle at high speed, heading for a playground. When a thing becomes possible, it is likely to become necessary. Now, the impossible seemed necessary. If I had any shred of decency, I would have to look into this business of war and violence from scratch, and pretty soon.

Not long after this I found a small group of students training in the way of the sword under a stern Sensei whose spirit was like bedrock. By some miracle I was allowed to join them.

MATTERS OF LIFE AND DEATH

4 THE DÔJÔ

The principles and applications of traditional Japanese swordsmanship have been accessible for hundreds of years. They are of practical relevance today for their effectiveness in self-mastery. This is a way, not of self-defense, but of self-discovery, and ultimately of true self-expression.

Training in *Budô* takes place within a dedicated facility, a building called the *dôjô*, or "place of the way." This is a component of almost all Japanese disciplines, not just martial arts. There are similar facilities in Chinese and Korean and other cultures. Probably they developed in Buddhist monasteries, where meditation and martial arts are still practiced.

The following describes one such facility:

The experience begins long before entering the building. We approach the front door on great stones, perfectly spaced. Gazing at the trees and the simple structure beyond brings a sense of expectant quiet. We might be ascending a remote mountain path. After crossing a wooden bridge, entering the doorway is like going into a forest. Stepping-stones continue among dark polished rocks and the sound of water. We think of what we may be carrying into this place, and what to leave outside. Light plays through green shoots. Across the still-yet-moving water, ancient and forbidding guardians come into view. Like the edge of a high mountain cliff, the atmosphere evokes heart-breaking beauty and abject terror. It is a turning-point admitting only those committed to the Way.

Climbing stairs, surrounded as by the timbers of some timeless stronghold, we emerge into openness and the sense of simple but serious purpose for which the entryway has prepared us. Much that is essential in architecture consists in what is not there: this is a laboratory of martial arts, and nothing else. Taking in the dimension and stillness of the space... the exquisite brushwork in an almost understated toknoma... the expanse of tatami... we bow toward the Shinza. It is time to get to work. Things that happen in the dôjô are only recalled like something seen from a moving train, if at all.

  -(about The Tômôn, built by Josh Freeman)

Entering a dôjô for the first time, one may be overwhelmed with the details of proper dress and deportment, and at first glance it looks as if students work unbelievably hard to gain the prestigious Black Belt signifying mastery of the art, after which life is more or less solved. The first assumption, the hard work, is quite true, although inevitably underestimated both as to one's own limitations and the lengths to which one will be required to go. But unlike the hierarchic educational approach of the western world, in which we ascend from novice to levels of greater privilege, always trying to get to somewhere else, in this discipline we strive to free ourselves from delusional thinking, in order to get nowhere.

It is probably just a coincidence that the word, nowhere, is made up of now and here. But now, and here, are exactly where the swordsman must be. The name for any other location is suki, sometimes translated as "opportunity," sometimes as "distraction." Far from being a mark of superiority, let alone mastery, rank is an obligation that entails enormous responsibility. At the lower levels rank is displayed so that others can know how much intensity you may be expected to handle safely. The coveted Black Belt is merely recognition that you may possibly be ready to begin serious study. Newly-minted *yûdansha* now belong to something much older and larger than themselves, and there is a large measure of being owned, as well as ownership in this term. More senior practitioners will not need belts or special uniforms to recognize one another, or to convey their authority.

In the western educational paradigm the student is a consumer of products, and acquires proof of purchase in the form of certificates and degrees; in the Japanese dôjô the student is a humble lump of dirt that may possibly contain ore of sufficient quality to be transformed into polished steel in the master's forge. There is a deep and profound transformation of a student's entire being. As with a newly forged blade, this is far from a certainty. Many a blade fails in the last stages of forging, and many a student fails to maintain the rigorous demands of this discipline. A master, under a master's defining obligation, goes to any lengths for the sake of the student, and the student, recognizing this, strives all the harder to make that enormous task less burdensome. It is this, and not medieval authoritarianism, that accounts for the extreme deference shown to instructors. It is expressed most profoundly in unusually intense concentration, attentiveness and focus in every aspect of living, whether in the master's presence or not. It is the only way to honor the debt incurred in such a relationship, short of carrying the tradition forth for others, and that obligation too will come with rank. In this way an unbroken chain is forged, linking the generations.

Japan was a highly refined civilization when the first waves of Europeans began the long invasion of what would become America. In seventeenth-century Japan, philosophy, science, literature and the arts were already as mature and well-established as in the great European cities. The literature of those times reflects a depth, originality, subtlety, richness and clarity that places Japan among the most refined cultures of the world.

No culture has escaped the darker aspects of barbarism and brutality, and in this the Japanese culture was no exception. But its contribution to what is best in humankind is profound and worthy of deep study.

It is often said that the modern diffusion of culture has brought decline. The martial arts have certainly been through a homogenizing process. Commerce and a revolution in communications have allowed for a wide but shallow public understanding of the ancient disciplines, at about the level of the cowboy mythology depicted in American film entertainments. Following World War II, journalists like Joe Hyams, for one of the better examples, trained under various instructors, and tried, in the language of their times, to explain their experiences. The Occidental mind, imbued with the triumph of American Know-How, found it insufficient to follow one path all the way through life; perhaps this was too much immersion in the culture of enemies so recently vanquished, or perhaps western journalists and academics felt they must retain a certain distance in the name of objectivity. Whatever their reasons, many of the English-speaking writers sampled as many arts as they could find. Thus Mr. Hyams became a student of Ed Parker and Bruce Lee, among many other famous practitioners, themselves products of an eclectic mix of disciplines. Hyams' training was Chinese, Korean, and Japanese, thrown together and stirred. Most western instructors spoke of this approach as "taking the best from all the arts of the Orient."

As a result many essential aspects that set one tradition apart from another have been lost to the western world. What remains is a jumble of impressions of mysterious and inscrutable Oriental techniques. In this context enlightenment is an Oriental curiosity of little interest outside of academic sociology and psychology departments, where it is carefully preserved like the dried specimen of some exotic bird.

Recent discoveries in neuroscience seem to place these matters in a new light. For example, we now understand that our perceptions, however realistic, are not the same thing as reality. At this writing the advertising industry is still far ahead of the scientific community on this point, but of course it seeks to take ruthless advantage of our susceptibilities rather than to discover our real nature. How long humanity will continue this odd self-parasitism remains to be seen.

Popular interest in the Japanese arts of warfare is still based on a fantasy of the invincible, ascetic lone warrior, wandering the world with little but his near-magical fighting skill and a pure heart. But there is a truth behind this heroic mythology in the form of a unique educational model and a body of profound knowledge developed over centuries, dealing directly with the essential questions of human being. Timeless questions that could not be more relevant today, regardless of one's ethnic or cultural background.

The disciplines of Zen and Swordsmanship adhere to similar training modalities. During the turbulent consolidation of Japanese feudalism, Zen monks followed a rigorous and austere practice that the military class seems to have found congenial. Some scholars have written that the feudal warlords used it as a convenient means of political control while others emphasize a certain philosophical affinity. The Samurai rank and file may have found Zen conducive to sanity in a time of prolonged, extremely bloody social upheaval spanning many generations. Although there was no single, consistent doctrine among the various Zen sects, much less among the varieties of Buddhism, Taoism, Confucianism and Shinto then converging like great rivers in the churning currents of political intrigue and social change, the monks' and the warriors' training methods were similar in important respects. Zen was about ultimate freedom; the military trained for ultimate power; in both, a hard physical regimen and relentless practice formed the path of realization. The two ways met on the same steep and inhospitable metaphorical mountain.

5 TRADITIONS AND TEACHING

The Japanese educational methods and means, tested and applied for centuries, were well understood and fully developed when Japan was still in a period of constant internecine warfare. Today there is no mystery about how to go about this form of training. The real problem is having access to an authentic tradition. This is only found in a true teacher: there is no other repository but a living master.

The marketing of martial arts did not begin recently, but accompanied profound upheavals in political and economic life during the Meiji Restoration, in the mid-nineteenth century. Extreme economic pressures on traditions that had been jealously guarded family secrets for centuries forced fundamental change on those that survived. Despite this a few of the old arts remain, with unbroken lineage extending centuries into the past. To speak of purity in this context is to tread on very uncertain ground. Such traditions share many characteristics of language, and even the most rigorously-guarded languages, if they live, must evolve. Authenticity is impossible to verify, and extremely unlikely. While the pure arts may not have been utterly extinguished, it is rare that a prospective student will be able to locate a qualified teacher by any means other than blind luck. But as if this were not discouraging enough, it is extremely unlikely that a rank beginner, even blessed with such luck, could recognize a master in any case. A better approach might be to cultivate an open, teachable attitude and let the master do the recognizing.

The relationship of master and disciple is not ideological or religious, though it does have its ritualistic aspects, but it is a bond beyond filial. When I met the man I was to address as Sensei, I could not possibly have known what this encounter would mean. It would be years before I began to understand the nature of this relationship, and after nearly three decades I am more than ever just beginning. It is not merely a commitment to a person but to a way of life. With time and hard work, we begin to recognize its true dimensions.

Authentic commitment will have everything to do with whether the relationship prospers. It could even be said that the quality of the student's commitment is a defining characteristic of mastery in a teacher. A good instructor would certainly take this view.

It seems to me that the distance from my level of understanding to that of my Sensei is, if anything, much greater now than it was when I first bowed in more than a quarter-century ago. Perhaps this is only a growing awareness of a distance that has always been infinite. Sometimes I have thought I could see, with hindsight, ways in which my Sensei had grown in his own comprehension of the art; but this is only a sort of parallax, a distortion attributable to my changing point of view. Parallax describes the difference between what you see through a viewfinder or a gunsight, and what is captured on the film or hit by the bullet.

The brain is a meaning-generator, and keeps trying regardless. It is impossible to go beyond one's own event horizon, so to speak. The idea of catching up makes about as much sense as flying by flapping my arms. On the other hand, from the first moment in training I found I was capable of things in Sensei's presence that I could not normally perform by myself.

In the very first class I was permitted to attend, after demonstrating a certain counterattack Sensei stood before me, wooden sword in hand, and attacked! It was like standing on the track in front of a speeding locomotive. Before I could think of what we had just been shown, he was an inch away, the blade resting across my throat. He demonstrated the footwork for me. He barked a command that I knew somehow meant, Again!

At that moment, something shifted. My attention focused in a strange way: not on my thoughts, which were in gridlock, but on my surroundings. It was as if I had been knocked unconscious, and I was just coming to my senses. I was thrust into the present moment by the force of danger. Before thought could form he was upon me. This time I, or to be precise, my body unencumbered by thought, executed the technique somehow, I have no memory of how. This time his wooden blade found only my sleeve. "More better!" he said, already moving to the next student. I bowed deeply.

He may have seen a trace of the raw material in me, that would be worth the trouble of heating and hammering into some semblance of a gentleman. I only knew that it was now up to me to bring everything I could to my training. If I held anything back, I knew the door would shut firmly in my face. It was never explained to me, or written anywhere, and yet it was as clear as an exquisitely cut diamond that this was The Deal. The peculiar thing about this arrangement was that it did not seem to involve him; it was an agreement with myself, in which I bore all of the responsibility.

I found that as a rule, in Sensei's classes, I was always able to continue beyond the point where I would ordinarily run out of breath. Coordination, balance, timing, distance and power were all quite noticeably improved when Sensei was there. In this way I was provided with a template, my bones and muscles imprinted with the proper way to execute techniques I would not be able to perform correctly again for months or years to come. I would not be able to mistake my performance for anything approaching the standard he set.

We might put it that, as in Physics, observing is a creative act; that the Instructor brings an observing within which students realize potential in an extraordinary way. When addressing me, Sensei seemed to be speaking to a person much more capable than the person I considered myself to be, somehow inhabiting my body for a little while. His authority – not a title but something innate – overwhelms self-assessments, which, like aching joints, have little to do with what is actually possible for the student. To describe this as high expectations is not quite accurate; he does not impose a conceptual view of the student based on some method of evaluation, but rather engages the student directly, without regard for that student's self-imposed limitations or outward presentation.

There may be a neurological phenomenon at work. We know that there are "mirror neurons" that have us mimic the actions of others. Just watching a football game, about twenty percent of your neurons match those of a player. Your throat may hurt after attending an opera. Brains have a powerful tendency to connect with other brains.

But this is not to say Sensei is playing a trick on us. The word, Sensei, means "one who has gone before." One must have made the journey authentically. There is no way to fake this. There is only creation, and another word for creation is mastery.

As with music there is also a distinction between interpretation and improvisation. In Budô these seem to merge in the performance. At the moment of action, we perform, not an interpretation of a kata, but the kata. This requires that the performance be absolutely per form. The only way this can work is when the interpretation and the improvisation are identical; in other words, when the rigorously prescribed series of actions in performance is an act of authentic and spontaneous self-expression.

This paradox does not seem so difficult to grasp when I think of a great musical performance. Only by getting the ego completely out of the way does the master violinist, for example, bring forth the fullest self-expression. In such an event, we realize a self other than the one we normally call "myself." That self is universal, and brings us into direct communication, or communion, with the composer, through the performance of a master. The self being expressed, then, is both the performer's and the composer's as well as that of the audience.

It is characteristic of great teaching that students experience an astonishingly heightened level of competence. It is as if we borrow this ability from a possible future self, under the gaze of a master who sees us without the filter of the mind's self-identity. During training we bask in this borrowed competency, while establishing patterns of movement in muscle-memory. It is then up to us to find our way back to that exemplary way of being, despite the fact that it leaves no trace in memory. Eventually, with perseverance, we may re-create it, and re-cognize it, but as an original act.

This kind of effect on others is a particular quality of the master swordsman: had I been an adversary, I have no doubt my talents would have been correspondingly decreased. In Budô this quality is called *Aiki*. While there is indeed an imminent coming-together of energies, it is best to forget about the soothing popular translations of the characters that form this word as "unifying energy" or "universal harmony". This is an insidious piece of hogwash, probably aimed at reducing barriers to market, perhaps because most parents are not thrilled about sending their Junior Samurai to learn to be more aggressive. For an adversary it is not unifying or harmonious at all, unless we mean an opponent is made to harmonize with the pavement. To be on the receiving end is more like feeling the ground shake at the approach of a mile-long freight train, or standing in the ocean in front of a very large wave. One has no desire to challenge such forces. The only consideration is how to get out of the way.

From a utilitarian point of view this might seem a desirable skill to acquire. But the realization of this is not a matter of acquisition. It has more to do with clearing away what is already there, and one of the first things to go is that very desire for it. Whatever we can conceive of as an object of want cannot possibly be the thing itself, for which we have no reference. Of course it is not, it is a symbol representing something else, a concept without any corresponding reality. All too frequently we envision things that do not have any actual existence. We imagine ourselves having obtained our object, even when there is no possible way to know in advance what it is, or how life would be then. This is probably the basis for market capitalism, if not human history.

If you are fortunate enough to locate a true teacher of an authentic tradition and be accepted as a student, you enter a unique relationship. You agree to abandon all that you know, in favor of what someone else knows. It will probably take five years or more, just to begin this process.

6 COMMERCIALIZATION

The rank growth of commercial enterprises purporting to provide the authentic secrets of ancient Oriental arts has fostered stereotypes of Oriental mystery. This in turn has created new markets based on these stereotypes. Most of these enterprises offer supposedly practical applications of combat techniques for self-defense. There is a range of product orientation, from health and fitness to professional sports training, with a general emphasis on fighting arts thought to be derived from ancient traditions. At best these products must have been adapted, if indeed they have any historical roots, to meet market expectations. They are certainly not designed to weed out a large proportion of new aspirants very early in the program, as seems to have been the case in early times. Then many students died in the normal course of training, and rival institutions engaged in bloody competition. This would never do in a modern studio with paying customers. One does not walk into a modern place of business only to wait for three days in the snow for an audience with the junior instructor, much less challenge the head instructor to a duel. Modern enterprises, confronting liability issues, have watered down techniques that were originally quite dangerous even in a rigorous training context. Inevitably, techniques are softer, the stakes are lower. The purpose has shifted, and not in a small way.

But this is not a new change. It probably took place before the opening of foreign trade between Japan and the rest of the world, while martial training was still the exclusive province of the feudal warrior class. After more than two centuries of military-imposed civil order, the need and wherewithal to support large private armies was much diminished, leaving a surplus of unemployed swordsmen. Merchants had more money than unemployed Samurai, and less appetite for fisticuffs. Strenuous and dangerous martial arts training would not have kept body and soul together for long.

As also occurred in Europe, where my great-grandfather obtained attractive facial scars at clandestine affairs of honor in his university student days, the outward goals of training had shifted from battlefield practicality toward proficiency at dueling in formal attire. Martial arts offerings were made more appealing to those who could pay. Weapons became much fancier and more expensive, and techniques for manipulating them more flamboyant. Protective gear and safer practice weapons and rules of sportsmanship proliferated.

Today it is no easier to sell the kind of rigor and austerity that marks old-school Japanese training. This is a complete way of life, not an exercise program, and it is hard. In feudal Japan it was designed to drive away all but the most ardently determined prospective students, and their lives were already harder than most of us can imagine. Those who remained were not being trained to defend themselves, but to defend their community at ultimate cost to themselves. They were training to be able to die on command. In the strict tradition of swordsmanship the fundamental question of training is brutally simple: how to meet death without preference or hesitation. That one question is the critical difference. That is what defines Budô.

Most commercial martial arts schools are based on an entirely different question: how can I make myself and my loved ones safe in a dangerous world, without being arrested or sued? As the basis for a martial art this is a crippling disease. It is not a question, but a statement disguised as a question. It says, in effect, that the world is inherently hostile, but its demands are negotiable. In reality there is no answer that can deliver on any promise of security, because there is no such thing and never can be.

The way of the sword was never designed or intended for self-defense. It was developed by and for people whose only possible choice was a life of service and self-sacrifice, whose only hope and aspiration was for a good death, that is, one reflecting the total selflessness and commitment embedded in the meaning of the word, Samurai. This may seem over-idealistic, but the wisdom behind it may emerge as we delve further into the matter.

Training in commercial schools isn't a bad thing, it is just a different thing. It is neither martial nor art. It has a different purpose and leads in another direction. In contrast, traditional training in Budô has nothing to do with self-defense.

Nothing can ever make us safe, just as nothing can ever make us happy. Safety and happiness isn't an attainable condition, but an attitude. In a traditional dôjô it is an unspoken prerequisite for admission to the building.

MATTERS OF LIFE AND DEATH

7 THE FALLACY OF SELF-DEFENSE

On close scrutiny, the proposition of self-defense quickly becomes absurd. What is Self? What is it we think we are defending? We defend the body under physical assault; we defend the ego when the self we imagine is slighted or challenged. But regardless of what we protect, what remains in the aftermath of battle? Is it the same self?

It is much more likely that we defend something under the delusion that it is the self. We cannot predict the future, but we often act on predictions of threats to a self we cannot define.

Neurologically, a human being's self is at best a pattern of electric impulses representing a self, in a pattern of electric impulses representing a world. Even keeping the body alive is no guarantee that the self will survive the encounter. In the effort to do even this much, we may have already lost life.

As a weapon of combat, the sword requires close proximity to the enemy, and provides almost no chance of escaping grievous wounds or death. To approach this study with a view toward self-defense is the very definition of insanity.

It may still be tempting at our cultural and historical distance – even if we're Japanese – to think that the original purpose was survival, but this can only be true in the broadest general sense: preserving an individual's life does not seem to have been considered. Absolute obedience and fanatical loyalty supported the rulers and thereby the community. Undue concern for one's own worthless skin would be the last thing anyone would want to be suspected of in that context.

For an individual fighter to deliver this level of self-sacrifice reliably takes more than mere indoctrination, he must identify so completely with his liege lord that his needs and wants become the ruler's needs and wants, his life the ruler's life. He must not only obey every command, he must be capable of anticipating them, even if the ruler should already be dead and defeated. For illustration, here is a legendary example: with the castle overrun and in flames, a man charged with protecting certain documents cut open his own stomach, removed his own intestines, and stuffed the waterproof packet in the cavity. Dying, he threw himself into a burning building. The papers were later found intact.

Even after the end of the Shôgunate there was a stubborn tradition in which vassals followed their masters in death. This persisted even in the face of imperial edicts banning the practice. Clearly this dramatic expression of faithfulness reflects a deep and quite authentic personal experience of community, felt profoundly by subordinate ranks in a thoroughly regimented social order.

If we understand this historical context it is plain that the question of how best to become invincible, through the lens of Budô, is really the question of how to attain ultimate selflessness. In the course of that inquiry one may encounter the true nature of Self. In Budô that encounter is not hypothetical, nor does it accept theoretical responses.

Popular entertainments continue to feed dramatic fantasies of personal triumph in a hostile world. In that imaginary world, becoming invulnerable seems a logical response. But of course it is a logic of dreams. Trying to be impervious to death, we can only succeed in making ourselves impervious to life.

8 TRUTH

In striving to cause a sword to do what it is perfectly designed to do, we bring to the job much else besides what is necessary and sufficient. It is not so easy to withhold this extraneous effort, but with relentless practice we separate reality and illusion, self and ego. Perhaps there is a lot of illusion per unit reality, a very low signal-to-noise ratio, but experiencing this difference, however small or great, is essential.

Things are not what they seem, and we almost always respond to the seeming as if it were the truth. The endocrine system is triggered as surely by illusion as by reality. Presence is out of bounds for the ego, which is constructed after sensory impressions are processed in the brain. Since "I" lives in the solidified past, and never in the fluid moment, the truth "I" knows can never be more than a representation after the fact.

But there may be other modes of experience in which there is no difference between what is apparent and what is real. It seems possible to narrow the difference. This is a transformative, rather than an informative process. Rather than take on knowledge in a linear, sequential or cumulative way, we train to bring about substantive change in knowing. We are not changing what we know, we are changing how we know.

In the arc of a cut there is no time to figure things out or make corrections: I must abandon what I know just to keep up. As a great master once said, "In life, understanding is the booby prize." After some months of intense study, students say things like, the more I learn, the less I know. Partly this refers to their growing awareness of how much more there is to discover than they ever imagined; but with increasing frequency, from the opening ceremony to the closing bow they simply aren't there at all. They retain what they learn as muscle-memory. Emerging from a strenuous session in the dôjô, the mind is curiously, refreshingly empty.

Traditional Japanese sword training involves sequences of movement that must be performed exactly according to a standard unchanged in hundreds of years. *Kenjutsu* is a physical art. In the beginning one is entirely taken up with tiny, proliferating details, forcing the body into compliance with the rigid, unforgiving forms. The finer the focus, the more details appear. A simple command to step and cut increases in complexity like a fractal equation. The principles involved are not affected by scale. At some point the mind can no longer hold enough variables. The superficial strategies of daily life are of no use here. The mind is revealed in the gap between the form and the performance. We may seem to narrow the gap, but only if the level of refinement is constant: there is always a finer scale, at which the gap is as wide as ever.

Kumitachi, kata involving two or more participants, are similarly choreographed. Precise timing and distance are essential to correct performance. Kenjutsuka must handle myriad details as in kata, but in addition must respond with, not to, adversaries. This is one case where two heads are probably not better than one. One is bad enough. Mental activity is not sufficient here, and more of it is only more insufficient.

What is required is a particular state of being. There are terms of art for this in the specialized language of Budô, whose meanings do not necessarily translate into English. "No-mind" or "Immovable Mind" or "Remaining Spirit" do not tell us anything. Such concepts are not useless, but they can only point to a truth that must be experienced personally.

With time and a lot of hard work, performance and form approach a degree of singularity. Two human beings move like a school of fish or a flock of birds in flight, unhurried and graceful, but faster than the processing speed of the brains that supposedly direct this dance. Attack is indistinguishable from counterattack. There is no self-defense involved, no self to defend. There is no more self-awareness or identity than could be found in a falling leaf.

MATTERS OF LIFE AND DEATH

9 WAR

In early agrarian societies the invention of granaries for storage of the harvest between growing seasons allowed a dramatic increase in the number of people a piece of land could support. This has far-reaching implications. There would have to have been an organized way to protect the community's stores in times of dearth. When people got hungry it would have been difficult to avoid consuming the next season's seed. It would not have taken very long to understand this relationship, and institutionalize something so directly connected to community survival. Religion might have had its origins in this, although there is now reported archaeological evidence to the contrary at sites of apparent religious importance frequented by bands of hunter-gatherers. In either case people would need some compelling reason to sacrifice themselves for the greater good. The priesthood might not always predict the planting season or the migrations of herds successfully, and rather than lose their seats, or some other part of their anatomy, they might blame capricious deities and suggest burnt offerings of most prized flesh to propitiate them. They would not have wanted to overdraw that account. Apparently they found that a little sacrifice in advance could go a long way, as well. Virgin daughters would do nicely, or perhaps the virgin daughters of people living over the next hill. Sooner or later burgeoning populations must meet, and competition and friction arise, and warfare technologies develop.

This is all conjecture, of course, about a possible variant on countless social experiments, a few of which left archeological traces, and only a small percentage of those were likely to have survived. One surely did, as we are living proof, and the above seems as reasonable a guess as any. However it happened, once warfare became organized, it sank deep roots in every culture. It remains among the most dramatically influential factors in the extraordinary acceleration of technological development, most of which has taken place within the last two centuries.

After World War II, General Douglas MacArthur declared that war is so destructive as to render it useless for solving disputes. But when we consider that our entire world has been shaped by war, solving disputes hardly seems a sufficient rationale. There seems to be much more at stake than mere disagreement among belligerents. It is more like a fermentation process in which individual human beings are but wisps of froth on the boiling surface. Everything we call Progress seems to have come from war. We have also refined the technologies of warfare to a precise science, pouring ever more of our wealth into research and development to the point where we can kill more people, with less effort, in a shorter time, from a greater distance, than ever before in history. Profit is no mere by-product, the always-enticing economic allure of violence has been refined along with every other technology of killing, to a numbers game. Hell is big business.

Yet popular language has remained amazingly stagnant, describing a world that has not existed for generations. To hear us talk, war might still be conducted on horseback. We speak about modern warfare in the language of the Arthurian legend, the Homeric epic, or the Viking saga, as if warrior heroes still fought each other hand-to-hand in order to add the reputations of their vanquished foe to their own heroic tales. There were times when this was the path to fortune and fame, land and titles, the singing of exploits around the cooking fires, so the children would want to grow up to become warriors too. Tales of warrior-kings glorified their names long after they had died. To attain power one had to face the enemy personally, and be seen doing so by those in command, which meant going in front of the front lines, where the commanders placed themselves. A code of conduct evolved to establish the immutable laws of honor, loyalty and courage, eventually. Thus, one way and another, we have the specialized languages of Bushidô and Chivalry. But these seem to have become orphaned linguistic domains without an underlying actuality. Modern warfare is conducted in a quite different language. It is highly technological and inaccessible to outsiders.

The rate of technological innovation and refinement continues to accelerate. The more radical changes that have occurred in the techniques of warfare, from hand-to-hand combat to mechanized industrial-scale destruction, took place within living memory. An elderly relative of mine faced the last cavalry charge in history. This tragic event involved, said that titled English gentleman, thousands of mounted Italian soldiers brandishing their sabers, riding at full gallop into heavy British machine-gun and artillery fire. The British were so taken aback at this that they were nearly overrun before they responded, but when they did it was with deadly finality. After the war was over, my relative and the enemy general, sharing a passion for horses, became lifelong friends. That battle was less than a century ago. Today, remotely controlled aircraft can place high explosives within a few feet of any location on the Earth's surface, and even several meters below it. The young pilots need never have participated in so much as a fist-fight, to ignite the very air over a mile of roadway, blanket a city with unquenchable fire, or render entire landscapes permanently uninhabitable.

Along with all of this very disruptive change, the machinery of economics has kept pace with the machinery of war. Transactions that once took months to complete, for wagon-loads of goods and the services of hundreds of people, now happen in units of time approaching the infinitesimal. In a similar way, too, the language of trade has not kept pace with reality. We speak about the reasons for market fluctuations as if it made sense to say "the market is nervous about Spain," or other such patent nonsense. People may be nervous about one thing and another, but computers respond only to sets of commands, some of which they now issue internally without human interference. It is as meaningless to speak about going to war to solve disputes as to talk about amassing great wealth in the marketplace with pluck and hard work and fair play.

Clearly the further development of technological warfare must reach a point of absurdity. Soon enough, beams of light from the sky will disintegrate any target, anywhere, without the possibility of defense. Possibly the targets will be other machines. The literary fantasy of machines set against each other, fighting on years or eons after the last human being has been vaporized, has already become quite feasible in reality.

In the face of all this, the universality of war, the question of its possible biological roots, and the accelerating pace of technological refinement, why would traditional training in swordsmanship persist for hundreds of years after the sword was obsolete? Why would the fighting arts of a long-vanquished feudal elite be anything more than an antiquarian hobby that could never sustain the practice more than a few years at best?

This training goes far beyond military technology, strategy or tactics. It deals with human being at the last frontier. It deals with Mind.

10 BEING READY

My Instructor stood me in front of the class.

"Assume a high block stance. I'm going to hit you on the head, like this."

WHACK!

"Do not let me hit you." With a shout of assent I complied, my arm and fist raised to protect my head.

WHACK! He slapped the top of my head again.

"Block! Protect your head!"

WHACK! "Concentrate!"

WHACK!

With his hand only inches from my defending arm, he continued slapping my head with complete impunity. It was not very painful, but even though I knew it was coming, and was already blocking the strike, nothing I could do was quick enough to deflect his hand.

"All right. Relax. Forget about defending yourself. Gaze into the distance. Think of nothing in particular. If anything happens, just imagine your arm floating up" – he moved my arm to suit the words – "and just be still." He began as before, slapping at my head from about a foot away. Suddenly I was very difficult to hit. Although I was standing normally, arms at my sides, pretty much ignoring him, my arm blocked every attack. I could not follow it. I did not will it to do this. My arm moved effortlessly, with speed and accuracy I did not know I had.

In that moment I did not learn how to do anything. On the contrary, I unlearned something. Up to that point in life I had always known – or thought I knew – that thinking is the essence of consciousness, and that learning must be a new thought or a change in thinking. But now, everything I knew seemed to contradict itself. I became aware of another way of knowing.

My idea of "ready" was not readiness; it was an idea, a representation of something – a picture of being ready. Trying to do what I imagined was required only rendered me helpless. My body was tense as I tried to locate a threat and counter it in time, an impossible task that left me utterly unprepared for any actual attack. Trying to do it better just made everything worse. Even the expected event was too fast.

When I stopped doing all those things associated in my mind with the idea of being on guard, letting go of any idea of defense, the attack seemed to come in slow motion, and my response was as unpredictable to me as to the attacker – but also, effective.

The brain is exquisitely developed for anticipating problems. It does this by recording whatever happens when we survive some situation. There are, of course, no records of the alternative. From these memories it retrieves likely responses to dangers it tries to predict. Memories are representations of past events, but when they arise, we respond as if thrust back into the actual situation. This seems to have been sufficiently effective for survival of the species, so far. But the process can also perpetuate the very problems it attempts to solve.

For example, my "on guard" attitude in the exercise could be a metaphor for airport security. It is not actual security, but an idea representing something we agree to call security. The system is inefficient in the same way my "ready" posture was, tying up resources that could be put to better use. Whether this is effective or not brings up the question, for what purpose? In life we win the games we are really playing. We do not always name them accurately, whether by design or through ignorance. If airport security is supposed to make the public feel safe, it has failed. But it may have other uses.

A threat is only an imaginary future constructed from bad memories. Responding to threats does not address any actual problem. While our minds are tied up in these compelling pictures it is impossible to deal effectively with actual events. Each time something untoward happens we add that eventuality to the list of things to make impossible, and tell ourselves we are safer. If nothing bad happens we call this effective security. We cite the infrequency of terror attacks as evidence that our policies are effective. This is like claiming that a crowing rooster causes the sunrise.

Ostentatious security measures are neither a deterrent nor an adequate counter to any actual attack; quite the opposite.

Training in the way of swordsmanship does not aim to improve security. There is no such thing as security. It is entirely conceptual. Instead, training aims to open the possibility and develop the habit of being present and engaged and aware, living in the most intimate and immediate way with the present moment. For this we must be open "on eight sides" to direct experience. Another word for that is "vulnerable". Ultimate readiness may be indistinguishable from ultimate vulnerability.

"For beauty is nothing but the beginning of terror..." — *Rainer Maria Rilke*

MATTERS OF LIFE AND DEATH

11 DEFINING TERMS

Budô (Japanese) *Bu* – war; *Dô* – way
Bujutsu (Japanese) *Bu* – war; *Jutsu* – art or technique

The implications of how we understand this word *Bu* reach into almost all of the terms and concepts now in common use in training facilities around the world. Although derived from Japanese, in American dôjô the popularly accepted definition of *bu* as "war" conveys only a small part of its meaning . Context does not come along quietly when we translate, especially between a poetic language and a prosaic one.

Once we have a word for some idea, it becomes a token. But words in one language may have no exact counterpart in another: the context within which one culture understands the meaning may have no relevance in the other culture. For example, to the Western mind *Jihad* is thought to be the Arabic word for "holy war". Like *bu*, this word leaves its context and most of its meaning behind when translated into English. To Arabic-speaking Muslims *Jihad* may refer to the individual's struggle to overcome bad personal habits, or feed one's family, or simply to persevere in the face of ordinary day-to-day adversity. The intention is to act in the right way despite circumstances or desires.

If we want to penetrate to the heart and essence of Budô we must either use the original language, or find translations that convey the full breadth and depth of original meaning. There are significant challenges involved. Using Japanese terms in the dôjô without exploration into the Japanese language inevitably reduces them to English jargon.

Who questions the meaning of a word once it finds its way into a dictionary? While it is true that Nelson's "Japanese-English Character Dictionary" defines *bu* as "military matters", there is a range of experience treated as essential in old texts, of which the people writing dictionaries may have been blissfully unaware. Even in translation, we can glean from the context in some of the old writings that in Japan five or six centuries ago *bu* could mean much more than war on the battlefield.

Thinking of peace as the normal state of affairs and war an aberration, or vise-versa, assigns the concepts of war and peace to circumstances. As a kind of weather report, "war" hardly fits the idea of "the Way of War," as in Budô. *Dô*, the Japanese pronunciation of the Chinese *tao*, implies much more about being on a particular kind of path, than about external conditions. Clearly *bu* has a broader meaning, and cannot be a direct counterpart of war, and to use it in that way obscures much of what our predecessors might have to teach us.

A better English word for *bu* might be "engagement," in the sense of being engaged completely with life now, in this moment. Budô and Bujutsu would be "the Way of Engagement" and "the Arts of Engagement".

The critical distinction between Bujutsu and Budô is often misunderstood. We read that *dô* is a spiritual Way and *jutsu* is technique or art. It is easy to conclude that one is philosophical and the other practical; but traditional practice approaches both through physical training. Zen, too, is a decidedly physical practice, not a mortification of the flesh by any means, but a method that deals with the mind through the body, and not through the intellect. In all cases we are required to engage, to immerse ourselves, to commit everything, actively, now. In Bujutsu the student strives for mastery of an unchanging set of forms that constitute the proprietary method for mastering techniques and strategies of a particular tradition. In Budô the student strives for mastery of the self. Broadly speaking, one is about action, the other being. Thus we pursue a way of being engaged (Budô) and this way is expressed in methods and techniques of engagement (Bujutsu). Budô may fairly be said to be the context within which we practice Bujutsu. In practice the spiritual sensibility emerges through the physical training, rather than through dogma, ritual or intellectual exercise.

In pursuit of the way there are no fixed rules or measurable accomplishments that place one in a particular rank; mastery in Budô is obvious the way mastery of the violin is obvious to the eye of another practitioner, and even junior students may experience a kind of awe in the presence of true attainment. On the other hand, a daunting level of rigor applies in Bujutsu. A very high level of mastery is theoretically possible without much technical proficiency, but one's performance in bujutsu will be limited without the foundation of Budô.

Total obedience is required of Bujutsuka. We must abandon all pretensions to any knowledge or autonomy, deferring to our seniors on every point; our opinion is not sought. One does what is expected without question or complaint, even when one sees no progress or purpose, much less consistency, in the instruction. This is not supposed to be an ego-friendly environment. It forms the background to thousands of repetitions of difficult training exercises. One does not worry about one's rank, that is up to Sensei.

In Budô, however, there is an element of spontaneity that both requires and challenges a high level of awareness. In both Bujutsu and Budô the Instructor's job is to develop the student, and the student's job is to make the Instructor successful at this demanding task, and be quick about it.

If Bu only means violent conflict, it implies that life is only at stake when we are in danger. But life is always and unconditionally at stake, every moment. Living is not guaranteed just because we have a pulse.

In one English translation of the legendary swordsman Musashi's "Gorin no sho" we find the instruction, "Make your fighting stance your everyday stance, and your everyday stance your fighting stance." In another the translator renders it this way: "It is necessary for you to have as your posture for strategy just the ordinary one, and it is essential that the posture of strategy be the ordinary one for you." As a new student I assumed that this refers to being on guard all the time, and would stand around in postures of studied menace. To anyone else this looked as ridiculous as it was.

Taking the broader meaning of *Bu*, Musashi might be telling us that being fully awake and alive in the present moment should be our ordinary posture, regardless of circumstances of war or peace.

12 MASTERY

There is nothing but this moment. Past and future are electronic pulses in our brains, right now. Whether or not there was or will be existence, it is pointless to aspire to great accomplishment only to die after a few dozen turns around the Sun. Where will all that accumulated wealth of knowledge and skill go then?

Perhaps as a byproduct of our mental complexity we invent, maintain and develop arts, science, literature, religion, agriculture and so on, far beyond what one lifetime could produce, much less comprehend. This body of work is not merely abstract or metaphorical. It may be the key to survival for creatures born naked and helpless, as practical as antlers or fangs or protective coloring, or the rigid division of labor that serves hive insects so well.

We know that whatever we protect as "myself" will end with death. No matter how good I get at defending myself, an end will come. A master without students can be no more than a good technician, and only for a few short years at best. A true discipline has a life of its own, independent of one person's life or concerns. In service to this larger purpose, in addition to skill mastery must include stewardship. If a discipline is not sustained by its disciples, it dies with them. A master is but one link in a chain, with all that the metaphor suggests about integrity, connection, constancy and purpose. No student or teacher exists in isolation: someone is on either side, senior to the right, and junior to the left. Sensei observes that only the Old Man himself and the newest *mudansha* have in common a certain coldness on one side, one seated in the chilly drafts by the door, the other next to the Void. The master's obligation and duty is to forge new links.

Mastery is not in the acquisition of the art's contents. Consider the sheer enormity of this project: after centuries of development there would be more knowledge than one person can possibly assimilate in a single lifetime. How is it possible to be a repository of all that the previous masters have added, much less to acquire facility with the infinite combinations of thousands of techniques? How can the art be maintained without loss across generations? In this unique educational system a master does not interpret the teachings, but becomes the source, and creates them anew.

Mathematicians and computer programmers use a term-of-art: Elegance. They mean a sort of poetic quality of economy and efficiency that is also inherently beautiful. During the process of their work there is sometimes a kind of collapse into elegance, in which complex sequences of logic suddenly condense to an irreducible essence. A page of equations or computer code may suddenly be expressed in one simple line; but this could not be achieved except through the complex process from which it emerged. In a similar way, the principles of an art may crystallize into a profound truth.

The scrolls awarded to students are an index to principles that have already been transmitted personally; they may also be a compressed form of information if considered in their full cultural and linguistic context. The student's own body forms a repository of knowledge without which the writings are only so much beautiful calligraphy. Mastery might seem to be measurable in terms of facility with techniques, but in reality one must be an original source of the art. A very good, very senior student may perform hundreds of techniques with exquisite skill. A master simply acts. One is a practitioner of an art, the other its very embodiment.

13 ART

In any art there is the problem of technique. Even artists who disdain technique must deal with it. I heard a fascinating discussion of this recently when master musician Philip Glass was interviewed. At one time he studied with Nadia Boulanger, the great French pianist and teacher. It brought a memory of my own very brief encounter with this formidable personage at the age of 12 or 13. After attending her performance I was able to reach her backstage. When she turned to me, her attention was like a searchlight. I asked what she thought of the new "synthetic" music. Turning to a man next to her, she asked, in French, what I might be asking about. He thought a moment and replied, "Ah – une automat." "Une ma-chine?" she asked, incredulous. Turning back to me, she looked again into my face. "It fr-r-ights me!" she said in her thick French accent. And the crowd closed around her, leaving me stunned, not with the trivial question, but that inescapable gaze, a personality so completely present and engaged, it was like a force of nature. When Glass said she had not been a nice person, but a great teacher, I think I know just what he meant. This was not a person whose time I would want to waste. Perhaps I may hope not to have done so.

Mme. Boulanger had taught Glass about the relationship of technique and style. It happened when she assigned him an exercise in harmony. He followed all the rules of voicing, and constructed the passage correctly. Still she shook her head. "But Mademoiselle Boulanger, every note is correct," he protested. "I know," she replied, "But it is still wrong."

Ancient Zen masters nod approvingly. Correct, but still wrong!

It was then, Glass said, that he understood what she was teaching him. "Before you can have a style, you have to have technique," he recalled. "It is the only basis for choice, otherwise you just have a series of accidents."

A potter I knew had a special wall next to the kiln. There was a pile of broken shards there. When the kiln was opened, he would examine each pot, and decide whether it had come out as intended. Ruthlessly he hurled many a beautiful accident against that wall.

It is difficult to transcend technique, to get beyond it to the realm of style, that which distinguishes a phrase of Bach from a phrase of Beethoven; but what about writing music that is not recognizable as one's own? In the interview, Philip Glass remarked that it is not a question of attaining a voice through technique. "It's getting rid of the thing," he explained.

Natural talent, knowledge, technique and virtuosity do not add up to mastery. Without it, creation is missing. Mastery is creativity itself. Nadia Boulanger needed no higher authority than herself, either to substantiate her teaching, or in providing definitive performance. It is the same in every field. A master has dispensed with all these trappings, and in fact, even the quality of physical equipment – the fine musical instrument, the specialized tools, the sword – is of little concern.

Picture if you will, a famous old music store in New York City. The young man behind the counter has a customer, a student of the saxophone, who is choosing a reed for his instrument. Reeds are chips of bamboo, shaved to a precise edge, and numbered by the resiliency of the finished product; this is the part of the instrument that vibrates, producing sound. To make sound depends on exacting conditions of moisture and temperature and pressure on the delicate bamboo reed in the mouth of the player. To make music is another matter.

This young man cannot be satisfied. There are a dozen open boxes of reeds strewn about the counter as he tries them out, showing off his advanced technique with elaborate fingering for a small audience of bystanders. He tests and rejects each one, impatient and imperious and dismissive.

An older gentleman has been standing quietly waiting his turn, and eventually the salesman turns to him and inquires as to his needs. He picks up a discarded reed, and turns to the student. "Got a quarter?" The youngster, clearly puzzled, hands over a coin. The man places the new reed across the coin, and flipping open a battered Zippo, proceeds to burn off the edge, down to the rim of the coin, scorching a rough, thick and jagged arc. He installs this charred wreckage in place of a good reed on one of the store's display instruments, and putting it to his lips, closes his eyes, and breathes into it. A long, rich, lyrical song emerges, so beautiful and moving that nobody can speak. The student, his face drained of color, pays for the nearest box of reeds and departs.

Similar stories abound in any art. A young upstart displays some fancy work, only to be exposed as a rank beginner from a direction he could not anticipate. In Zen it is the classic *mondo* conversation called "Dharma Battle" about which there are scrolls twelve centuries old for Zen monks to batter themselves against in pursuit of enlightenment.

There is a gate at every stage, and no getting around it. Technique is one such barrier. There is a world beyond technique, of pure expression. We begin by attempting to do Art in hope of becoming an Artist. We magnify small accomplishments. At this stage it is about "me" and "my" skill and prowess. Many remain here, endlessly polishing technique and perhaps dazzling some admirers. But technique is only the beginning.

Art is an expression of Self. There is no becoming anything, only being. An Artist needs Nothing to create art. This Nothing, however, is not so easy to come by. It may come at a very high price, after years of grueling work; or as a gift outright; or never.

The way is not the content of teaching or a catalog of techniques. These may help to put your feet on the path, but are not the path itself. Ultimately there is no path until you step forward.

14 SATORI

There is nothing that so focuses the attention as being within the arc of a moving blade.

On a certain day, I arrive at the dôjô and change into my uniform. I enter the tatami and kneel. I bow toward the *shinza*, and all that remains of the world outside is some sense of the season, perhaps gentle rain on the roof, or bird songs, or wind in the bamboo. I assume the posture for *zazen*. Not in silence, exactly. In stillness.

On this occasion someone will be photographing what we do, so the usual class format is suspended, but I do not expect to be taking a major part in the proceedings. Taking up *bokken*, we perform some kumitachi, and then begin a kind of un-scripted sparring.

In the dôjô, whether training in Zen or the sword, even those who have great strength and stamina confront an essential problem: everything we are conscious of has already happened. It is a cold neurological fact. At best we are a moment behind events. Training can improve response time significantly, but no matter how quickly we learn to react, the present is always just out of reach. We can't seem to get here from there. And in both disciplines, here is where the action is. That this is a matter of life and death goes without saying in the martial arts, but in the contemplative traditions of Zen it has been phrased like this: Zen is a matter of life and death!

In addition to their *makimono* of techniques, accomplished masters have left volumes of general instruction for their students, among whom were legendary heroes and generals of medieval history. They do not detail teachings that were intended for direct transmission, but still get straight to the point. "When in doubt, choose death!" they write. "Throw away your life without hesitation." Surely they meant something other than to lie down and die. What, then, is "choosing death?" What is "your life," and how could you throw it away?

Consider the following: the world you know as real, a world of meaning created against a background of remembered experiences, everything you think of as yourself – all that you call your life – is all that stands between you and being fully alive in the present moment.

It seems nearly impossible to speak about enlightenment and make any sense. We talk about it. We have shelves of books about what it might be like. Implicit in our way of speaking is the assumption that it can't happen here, now, to me. But this is absurd. How could presence ever be other than here and now? For centuries, great masters have devoted their lives to point out that in fact, it can only happen here, now, and only to you.

In the present moment, things are, if they are, and if not, not. This is the natural state of human being. The old texts dismiss the idea of elevating enlightened persons to exalted status. They also indicate that such direct experience reveals both our delusive thinking and the eternal truth of our real nature. They warn us against becoming enthralled in the experience, urging us not to tarry, lest truth devolve to yet another belief in yet another concept. Belief is alright, but it is not presence. Understanding is of no use here, what matters is performance.

"I" is a thought, not the thinker. Most thought perpetuates "me". But sometimes the constant internal monologue is forgotten – and "I" ceases to exist – in the heat of a moment. We submerge again into "normal life" and say it was luck, divine intervention, a peak experience, anything but ordinary, pure, focused attention. Anything but performance. The mind replaces what happened with a plausible story so quickly it escapes our own notice.

There is a state of presence that can be experienced with a simple experiment. Sit face to face with a partner, hold eye contact, and both shout as fast as possible, all the colors you can think of. You may repeat a color, unable to think fast enough to choose at random; just keep shouting as fast as you can, at the top of your lungs. Quite suddenly you may find you have been shouting the same sequence of colors simultaneously.

In combat it may seem paradoxical that two brains committed to destroying each other should entrain in this way, but terror and love are not so far apart on the scale of human experience. In what other circumstances do human beings pay such close attention to one another? Surviving veterans sometimes report a sense of intimate connection to the enemy, in the midst of murder and death, as in the following poem by A. E. Housman:

I did not lose my heart in summer's even,
    When roses to the moonrise burst apart:
When plumes were under heel and lead was flying,
    In blood and smoke and flame I lost my heart.

I lost it to a soldier and a foeman,
    A chap that did not kill me, but he tried;
That took the sabre straight, and took it striking,
    And laughed and kissed his hand to me and died.

Maintaining all the illusions we present to the world, let alone the other illusions we fervently believe in, takes a lot of energy. From day to day I keep track of a vast array of potential cascading disasters. The brain seethes with calculations: how do I look to other people? What do they think of me? Are my clothes disarranged? Is something stuck between my front teeth? Do they know about the candy I stole when I was four years old? How (ugly, foolish, charmingly silly, inauthentic) they look to me! What inane conversations they are having! And this is merely what happens when an ordinary person enters a pleasant social gathering among friends.

Who – or what – is thinking these thoughts? And just try to stop this stream of so-called "consciousness." We expend all this energy for one purpose, survival. But this "survival" is not necessarily the same thing as avoiding death, it is survival in the world of the mind. It is the perpetuation of an idea, an identity. In our mental model of the world, the symbol of "myself" encounters symbols of "danger" and "survives." This virtual "self" is more concerned with the appearance of conforming to social norms than keeping the body alive. It will sometimes even sacrifice the body in order to preserve this idea of "myself."

Most of us are in various stages of dying, quickly or slowly, to sustain a self-image. Just whom do you think you are? That is the "self" the mind is at such pains to preserve. If it fails in this – but it never does. How can it fail, while the lights are still on? Whatever happens becomes the latest definition of survival. And so we persist in thinking we have escaped yet once more. That anyone is truly alive is open to serious question.

The ancients use the metaphor of a gateway between the world of the mind, and present actuality. We can only pass this gate after giving up what seems as real and definite a self and as precious a life as ever was. Yet something has a death-grip on something it considers life.

Wooden swords provide no margin of safety. The danger of irreparable injury is actually greater than with razor-sharp blades. Severed parts may sometimes be restored by modern medical technology, unlike pulverized bone and muscle. The traditional wooden weapons save costly damage to an expensively polished antique. On this occasion we have some swords provided by a smith for testing. Damaging them will not matter. It is a rare opportunity.

We bow, and brandishing polished steel, without a word, at no particular moment we move in. We are utterly exposed and committed, here and now, without appeal to past or future. I had not expected to take part in the proceedings, and as it turned out, this "I", with its schemes for success, its secret embarrassments, everything else dear to "me," did not. Something happened without analysis or memory or anticipation, without "me." Also absent was every false refuge from the bright uncertainty of living in the present moment: violence, peace, danger, security, hope and fear.

MATTERS OF LIFE AND DEATH

15 AWARENESS

What is our real nature? This old Zen question is a very practical and purposeful one in Budô. It confronts us at every turn. Answers in language tend to seem absurd.

Life happens like a series of reflections in a mirror. All the activity of consciousness, the business of daily life, logic and language, thinking and speaking and listening, and also what we normally think of as "myself", is the reflection, and to be reflected, something must already have happened. The mirror in which all this is reflected does nothing, has no desires or preferences or attachments. Desire and attachment and preference are more of what it reflects, along with suffering and violence. Like a mirror, awareness does nothing; wants nothing; influences nothing. A mirror does not reflect itself.

We sense temperature, pressure, sound, smell and light before there is any meaning. If my hand touches fire or boiling water it reacts before I know hot from cold. Self-consciousness comes much later, by some fraction of a second, the reflection produced after processing the raw information from the senses.

In that case, who or what are you? If you are the one who appears after something occurs in the brain, how is it possible to be in the present moment? We can't know about the present moment until it has come and gone. There is no catching up. Before we know it things may go badly.

In swordsmanship there is said to be *mushin*. Translations fall short once again. It is something like getting behind the mirror of awareness. In the present moment, there is no reflection as yet, no language and no understanding. There can be performance, however, if its source is upstream, as it were, of the meaning created as the mirror image. Performance is reflected too, but by the time "I" understand what is going on the action is over. This is why, after kata or kumitachi, there may be no memory of what has happened. The kenjutsuka must operate in a moment that has not been processed and reflected upon. It is pure action.

Is it possible that we can have immediate experience without calculations of gain and loss, hopes and fears, evaluations and comparisons and decisions – and continue to function? Can life go on without the stream of thoughts that passes for "you"? What about being aware in a state of unknowing? Who would you have to be then?

16 ATTENTION

I recall standing watch on a square-rigged sailing vessel at night, steering by the wind. Clear moonlight and a universe of stars, we might well have been sailing through outer space. Other than responding automatically to wave action and the myriad small variations requiring slight corrections, there was no significant change that would interrupt the rhythmic monotony. When I was relieved just before dawn, I could not recall anything since taking the helm four hours before. Our wake was straight, the set of the sails perfect, our course true. Somebody had been steering quite well, and I had not left my post, but I wasn't there, for all I knew. My body had performed well. The only thing missing was my thinking and memory. Attention had been paid. Who had paid it?

Attention is elusive. If anyone had asked me if I was paying attention, who would have answered? Would I have started an internal monologue about the set of the sails, the feel of the water, the compass bearing? Every experienced mariner can recount at least one episode when all this was in order, and suddenly there was an unexpected event. Something had escaped attention. A large creature below the surface, or a sudden change in the wind. The other case is also common: there is a kind of attention that allows deep sleep, even at sea. I have awakened in the dark knowing from the sound of the waves against the hull that the anchor was dragging. One fine Sunday morning, in the dead of Winter, I woke up to find myself standing naked on a dock with the frozen end of a broken line in my hand, holding my boat as she rose and plunged like a wild horse in heavy storm surge. The line keeping her off the rocks had frozen solid and parted. I had jumped out of a warm bunk and saved the boat in my sleep. It was the stinging cold that woke me.

What we normally call attention seems quite the opposite. When we are thinking, attention is on our thoughts about the world, not the world. When another speaks, I hear my own thoughts about their words, not their words. Other than accidental episodes that occur in some kind of fugue state, we know nothing about attention. We speak as if we direct our attention, even while it is just as likely that attention is directing us.

Of course it is absurd to try to direct attention by thinking. In Zen, where body and mind are not treated as separate objects, breathing is found to have something to do with the focus of attention. It is not necessary – self-defeating in fact – to try to remember to pay attention to paying attention, only practice the physical technique of zazen, sitting and breathing correctly.

In Budô thinking is considered more or less a nuisance. When cutting, there must only be cutting.

17 KIME

Attention is critical in Budô. As a distinction, *kime* encompasses much more than what happens to occupy consciousness at a given moment. It is useful to remember than in Zen, body and mind are not two things. Focus, in this case, applies to the entire being. Kime is a requirement in all performance.

There is a wonderful scene in Kurosawa's famous film, "The Seven Samurai," in which the warriors recruit Samurai Number Three or Four. They hear his voice first, recognizing a proper *kiai*, and peer around an enormous pile of firewood. A man with an ax is setting up logs and addressing them like the swordsman he is, and dealing an impressive stroke. When he sees his observers, he carefully moves his sword out of reach, smiling a friendly greeting. Introducing himself, he jokes: "Woodcut School."

For several years I have lived in a rural area on an old farm that never had been wired for electricity or central heating. It was also located in a northern region with long, cold winters. I had to cut a lot of firewood. Fortunately there was a lot of forest, but firewood has an economy all its own. The saying, "Wood heats you twice" is a sorry underestimation. It heats you when you cut the tree; it heats you again when you saw the logs to length; it heats you again when you load it, and again when you unload it; and then you are halfway to a cozy evening by the fire. But all this preamble is to get to splitting.

Splitting wood by hand is similar to cutting with a sword, with significant differences, but it is a perfect laboratory for kime, at least at the elementary level. There are legends: Tesshu would be sitting zazen and notice mice falling out of the rafters dead, flies dropping out of the air, etc. Here I want to describe something a little more accessible to the beginner.

Most people, even experts, when splitting, driving a wedge, sinking a fence-post or a drift-bolt, or just impressing the ladies at the ring-the-bell attraction at the county fair, will do the following: taking up the maul with the left hand at the end of the handle, the right just at the hammer head, start the heavy end moving backwards, away from the target, sliding the right hand to the left as it gains momentum in a full circle, finally tensing every muscle just before impact – hopefully on the target.

A variation I've encountered, with a group of trained martial artists, is to start with the ax vertical along the backbone, head down, and use abdominal muscle and weight to bring the hammer down on the wood. While somewhat imprecise – and dangerous to bystanders – this is a slight improvement over the carnival swing.

After splitting seven cords every year for five years – a cord is 128 cubic feet of wood – I can say with some confidence that neither method will get you very far through a pile of chunks. For one thing, they rely mainly on the weight and velocity of the tool, which has a finite potential energy. For another, they require a tremendous amount of energy that does not add to the cutting power, in fighting centrifugal force, maintaining balance, and trying to land the thing somewhere near the wood. In effect, the lumberjack or the carnival rube is working much harder just to get the metal up in the air, hang onto it, and correct its trajectory. Control is disadvantageously sacrificed for power.

The method I use is directly related to swordsmanship. The splitting maul is a six-, eight- or ten-pound sledgehammer, with a blade designed to apply force laterally on impact. But it is a blade, and cutting action – motion along the edge – reduces the angle of the edge, and this makes a surprising difference. Also, instead of cutting a log on the ground, I place it on a chopping block about waist-height. But the important thing here is swinging the thing.

I grasp the handle as our exemplary lumberjack does, but with the right hand just guiding the ax along the vertical axis in front of me. I turn my hips right, thrusting upwards, so that the ax moves quickly up, and back about fifteen degrees from vertical. Without stopping this motion, the left hand is now pulled by a strong leftwards hip rotation, while the right hand pushes outward from my center, connected through shoulder and right hip to the turning torso. There is no sharp corner as the ax-head goes over the top. There is acceleration as the ax approaches the wood. There is no loss of control at any point.

The ax moves through about ninety-five degrees of arc. All of my effort feeds the momentum and velocity of the ax-head, while maintaining alignment in the arc of the cut – there is no sideways moment, and no correction needed. The wood explodes, or falls apart, or the hammer is buried in it, if it is something dreadful like silver birch (that's what hydraulic splitters are for!). Breath is everything; but more on that subject elsewhere. Body mechanics, ergonomics, and focus concern us now.

Let us return to kime. With constant practice – and the approach of Winter, like death itself, urging me on – I began to experiment with focus. Each muscle, each breath, each thought, footwork, the terrain, anything in the environment came under close scrutiny. And after awhile I found that there is a moment before the cut begins, when I know exactly where the blade will strike the wood, and precisely how the wood will respond. If I want six pieces out of a section of tree, I make three strokes that split through, but leave the log intact; and on the final stroke, everything separates into my six. If I want kindling, I add a little something to the body rotation, pulling or pushing the blade imperceptibly, and slice off thin sticks from the chunk, and it may rock, but does not fall off the block.

The moment – that instant before I begin to breathe and raise the ax – is not a calculation. It does not seem to matter whether I am feeling focused, or energetic, or lethargic and lazy. In that moment, I just know this piece of tree is about to become firewood. It has nothing to do with effort. It happens sometimes almost as an afterthought. I think this might be kime; when it is present, the wood is going to split as easily as a sigh.

There is almost never an effort, or a special wind-up, or a moment's meditation. Old men have a phrase – "holding your mouth right" – that is as good as anything to describe the presence of *kime*. Thinking about it, trying to do it, getting ready, anything I do will only chase it away. Odd as it might seem, my so-called attention wanders where it will in the course of an afternoon's splitting. It is pleasant, relaxing, refreshing work.

This is all very nice. But the mice in the attic and the flies on the window blithely ignore my ferocious meditations. We employ fly-swatters, and two cats.

18 VIOLENCE

There seems to be very little to say about violence beyond this simple, possibly astonishing truth: there is no such thing. Violence is not inherent in a situation or circumstance. One witness may describe an event as violent, while another may not. Violence is an interpretation of what happened, not what happened. We respond to the idea of violence as if it were what it represents. It is not: it is a word for an idea about an event in the past. The idea is not the event, it is a symbol. And it is not like a tree or a stone, objects that have reality in a way that a past event does not. The tree that comes to mind when you read the word may still be where you left it; not so, remembered violence.

Knowing this does not seem to help very much when the chips are down. This has something to do with the way conceptual representations of events are related to actual events. For most of us, most of the time, our interpreted world is identical with the actual world – or identical enough to get by. We respond, and the endocrine system responds, to the interpretations our brains generate. Rigorous training solves this problem, not by analyzing what is really going on, but by providing an alternative to the automatic interpretation of sensory information, and this alternative is not some better or different interpretation: it is non-interpretive.

We are so bound to the cause-and-effect way of seeing the world that adopting another way can seem very much like throwing away life itself. But recall the admonition, "choose death!" This may tip us off that we are still clinging to life instead of being alive.

Various experts have written about a built-in switch somewhere inside us, saying we can learn to throw that switch at the right moment to respond to violence appropriately. This theory, often expressed by very proficient fighters, can be misleading, so let us dispense with it here. There is no control panel that puts us in some kind of total fighting mode.

When patterns of brain activity recorded during previous traumatic experience are re-invoked, triggered by some similarity to present events, the brain assumes the same state it had been in during the recalled experience. When this occurs, we are not aware of the difference between present and past. As far as the mind is concerned this is a good survival strategy, since I survived the last event of that kind. In fact, any event I survive is treated not as a narrow escape, but as a method of survival. There is no neural record of any experience that I did not survive.

This is all a brain can do. It is the system we have at birth. Its function is to trigger a response somewhat likely to be relevant in the next instant. It is a crude sort of prediction device, but it can only make predictions out of what has happened in the past. This is not exactly a program for learning new things. It might be a fruitful area of study if we want to understand why abusive relationships, whether bad marriages or world wars, seem so persistent.

In Japanese swordsmanship we are not training to trigger reactions of that kind. There are, no doubt, many martial arts systems that do. In the way of swordsmanship we are training to be directly engaged with life, so that we act appropriately to present reality. When thus engaged, "I" is remarkably absent.

Being un-enthralled by a mental construct of the world, freed from the heroic internal narrative of one's imagined life, is at the heart of Budô. It is not preparation for combat, but an end in itself. It has nothing to do with war at all, in the usual sense. It is that state of being in which we are not subject to the delusion that our mental representation of reality is the world. Violence has no meaning in that realm.

MATTERS OF LIFE AND DEATH

9 FEAR

Think of a time when you were suddenly confronted with danger. The phrase, "jumping out of your skin," is wonderfully poetic. Perhaps you lost your footing at the top of a high staircase, or saw a snarling dog running toward you. What happened? You probably felt your skin intensely as if each hair was suddenly magnetized; there was a sharp intake of breath; you froze for a moment; then your arms flew up in front of your face, palms outward, fingers spread; knees snapped together, shoulders hunched, head ducked, hips twisted sideways. All this and more happened before you had a coherent thought.

The body protects its vital organs, interposing less critical parts to protect your head and torso, preparing for the worst even before your brain has time to assess the situation. Fright occurs as physiological changes. The mid-brain seizes control, bypassing the confusion and delay of perception and analysis. In training, rather than try to suppress this mechanism, we begin with a controlled situation and introduce variables carefully. Soon, like war horses, we become acclimatized to uncertainty.

We perceive the world very much according to what we expect. When something happens we react to some likely variant of expectation, rather than responding to what happens. But expectation is of little use as a guide in dealing with the kind of uncertainty introduced in the dôjô. My experience "being ready" is an example of this. Expecting to be struck in a certain way only interfered with effective response, even though the attack was exactly as expected.

Normally the mental model of the world around us includes most of the significant features, as well as a representation of oneself. If a sudden event occurs that is not part of this model, all of the body's alarm systems may fire, and we experience fright. Since all this activity is automatic, it is easily hijacked by an opponent. A simple feint to the eyes may render a person momentarily helpless.

Since we cannot anticipate what we don't already know, what we're afraid of can only be from our personal history. We cannot imagine what we probably should be afraid of, having no previous experience of it. Our worst fears have already happened. Still we persist in being afraid of a small set of events that are over, if not actually done with.

If there is no symbol of a self, and no mental model of a world, there is no automatic threat-assessment. There is no reaction, only presence. But one does not just stand there to be cut down. In the state known as *mushin*, a person is very, very hard to surprise, and free to act without hesitation, spontaneously.

From the standpoint of an attacker, who generally speaking has something very specific in mind, to encounter someone in such a state is like having the ground disappear.

20 BREATH

Unless something goes wrong with it, we take breathing for granted most of the time. In treating a person found unconscious, there are just two things to look for: breathing and movement. If breathing and movement are absent this is called "no signs of life."

There is no question that without breath, there is no life. However, once we embark on almost any true discipline, the breath becomes critical to performance. This is a highly refined aspect of both Zen and swordsmanship. It is at the very essence of practice in zazen, and in sword training every form begins and ends with its prescribed way of breathing. It is the foundation of the art. It is the key to movement, attention, power.

My introduction to breath power came years before I ever thought of training, while splitting a tree stump, working with two other men. After removing a tree in the city, the stump must be cut six inches below the pavement and cemented over. This was accomplished by the ancient method of sledge-and-wedge. The old man, our employer, tapped a steel wedge into a crack, and I swung my hammer with all the strength I could muster. This had no more effect than a raindrop. The huge man we called Tiny was next, arms and legs like tree trunks, his ten-pound hammer a toy in his massive hands. He smashed that wedge halfway into the wood with a blow that shook the earth. Then the old man raised his hammer about shoulder high and seemed to drop it, with a deep sigh, as if he had no strength left at all. But the wedge buried itself out of sight in the wood.

Unlike Tiny, who was too heavy, and the old man, who was no longer limber enough, I could climb the trees we were taking down, but the art of the sledge hammer eluded me. Eventually I could at least hold up my corner of the rhythm, striking in sequence, if not actually moving much metal. If I synchronized my breath with theirs just right, we became a smooth, mindless hammering machine. Working with these men, one impossibly strong, the other almost entirely a ghost, I did not exactly learn about breath power. It was more a matter of gaining ignorance: knowing there was something beyond my comprehension was an advance over complete blindness.

The first thing I learned when I began training was that I didn't even know how to breathe! This is something one must come to terms with in this discipline, this process of un-learning. At first it seems like there is a vast mountain of useless, irrelevant, hard-won knowledge that must be undone. With practice it becomes clear that most of what we call learning is really the replacement of one set of assumptions with another. But in traditional training it's all un-learning: we replace what we thought we knew with nothing. One day it is possible to be so emptied-out of all that infinite wisdom that present reality – to which we had been unaware that our assumed knowledge had blinded us – may appear. But meanwhile, *keiko, keiko, keiko*! Practice, practice, practice!

Breathing techniques emphasize use of the diaphragm and abdominal muscles, rather than expanding the chest. We do not see the shoulders rise and fall. Tidal volume, the amount of air exchanged in one breath cycle, is much higher with abdominal breathing, so that the body's demands for oxygen and the removal of toxins can be met at very high efficiency.

A cut begins with breath. From the center of the body to hips and legs, shoulders and arms, instead of lifting the sword up and pulling it down, an elegant, effortless, fluid motion comes naturally as one action, driven powerfully by breathing.

Breath is also the basis for relationship (all parents know this: it comes to you in the small hours of the child's birthday). Whether I breathe with my opponent or not is fertile ground for discovery. Rather than following eye movements or other possibly deceptive indications, in awareness of breathing we are attuned of the source of action even before the body moves, before the thought of moving arises. This can form such an intimate connection that it is even possible to assume command of an enemy.

We forget about breathing, and like the heartbeat it continues, but unlike the heartbeat, we can control it precisely. When we do not control breathing, other influences can change the rate and depth, such as the emotions of fear, sadness, joy, anger, and so on. This works both ways: actors report that "getting the breathing right" is a reliable way of simulating a character's emotional state.

We are provided with an automatic survival mechanism, but not a particularly sharp or precise one. That sharpness and precision is up to the individual, it is amenable to willful development. Breathing has much to do with how we experience life in a given moment, and our actions correspond to what we believe is happening. To regulate breath is to regulate the entire being. Breathing allows the ego to fade into insignificance. We empty the mind, still the inner voice, abandon desire and delusion, and just remain. Open on all sides. Present in this moment. Free to act directly, without hesitation.

MATTERS OF LIFE AND DEATH

21 TECHNIQUE

In Kenjutsu every smallest movement has a practical reason. As a new student, after months trying to perform the most basic movements of drawing the sword, the complex series of hand gestures seemed quite oddly stylized and impractical. Finally I asked.

Sensei addressed a senior man – in rank, not age – on my right. "Don't let him draw his sword." That substantial gentleman clamped his vice-like left hand onto my right wrist. "Hajime!" barked Sensei. Begin! I made the same gestures I had been practicing, and light dawned: The sword slid easily into my hand as if nothing unusual were happening. My upper classman, a burly policeman, was bent awkwardly off balance.

Techniques of this kind, observed assiduously in practice for all their apparent strangeness, are not at all unusual. This accounts for some rigidity of form aimed at preserving correct practice at a stage when students will not be capable of taking in such an overwhelming amount of detail. We move from general to specific, laying down the foundational points, and then sharpening focus.

Sometimes it seems as if Sensei is suddenly and capriciously altering techniques just when we get them right. In reality he is rewarding our efforts – sometimes after years of study – with a deeper teaching. I have the notion there are really several distinct arts, depending on one's level of comprehension: the beginners' version must be cohesive and effective to a certain degree, but it is far from the totality of the art. Thus there are many things very senior practitioners who leave the ryû will never be aware that they don't know, and sadly, there are many martial arts enterprises headed by instructors of this caliber.

In all likelihood many ancient arts have become useless when the underlying principles were forgotten, leaving only strange behaviors whose meaning is lost. The degradation of certain arts to mere exercises decorated with pretty embellishments is all too common. In some schools there are techniques practiced with certain small movements omitted so that instead of destroying the shoulder joint or breaking the neck, the technique is quite a pleasant experience. There are generations of advanced practitioners in sword schools whose weapons are beautiful fakes. While such practice is no doubt a lot of fun, it is not much good at making clear for students the dimensions of the mind.

Among other reasons, to prevent replicative decay *Reishiki* is the essence of the Ryû. Often translated as "right conduct," or "proper etiquette," Reishiki is an entire way of seeing the world, in which it is unthinkable for a mere student to do other than follow instructions precisely. As students progress the esoteric meanings reveal themselves, but meanwhile a large volume of information is taken in without the need for analysis or memorization, being directly written into the body. Explanations, should they be needed, may occur to the student later, probably years later. Maybe when they decide to write a book.

At a certain stage the student finds that questions answer themselves as they arise. Soon each session in the dôjô brings spontaneous insights in rapid succession. If students maintain a correct attitude, they learn how to learn in this way, and not to reject information just because it may appear extraneous or impractical on the surface. They become practiced in listening for the actual instruction, rather than their own internal commentary on what they hear. They begin to learn with the eyes.

Technique has been described as a ladder, to be discarded after we have climbed it. Without it, we cannot perform properly, but technique is not enough for mastery. A poet who can construct perfect couplets, but cannot induce tears, is unfinished as a poet. Technique is necessary but not sufficient. Some things are universal to all true Arts. When the great Maestro Leon Kirchner was asked about one of his famous students, 'Cello virtuoso Yo-Yo Ma, the old master fondly recalled the following episode:

"I was a severe critic, but only because even then I was in awe of him," said Mr. Kirchner. "I was always telling Yo-Yo that he didn't have the true center of his tone yet. Meaning there was something more spiritual, the center of his person, of his being, that was not coming through yet. Well, in 1976, Rostropovich came to ... do a master class... When Yo-Yo began playing for him, he stopped him and said, 'You know you have no center to your tone.'..."
– *Janet Tassel, Harvard Magazine, March-April 2000*

A Master Class is like a spirited mondo session. It is a high-level conversation, understandable only to those whose depth and maturity allow them access to the subtler aspects. But it is not abstract. The students dare not bring forth anything short of absolute, undiluted excellence; and the master's mere presence will try them like a hot forge.

MATTERS OF LIFE AND DEATH

22 BODY

In training the whole person, the most direct route is through the body. The sword arts are primarily physical arts. A central objective is to train oneself to perform efficiently, all parts in alignment. Reading or attending a lecture cannot approach the sheer density of physical experience. The information thus retained is far richer than a set of abstract concepts, and more immediately accessible. In a physical art, information is stored by making new connections in the intricate neural web of our brain and nervous system. Principles are put into the system through repetitive, constantly corrected and refined movement. Those principles are then available as needed in all other domains of life.

Conceptual knowledge may be synthesized from this training, but seldom if rarely does it work the other way around. If this is not clear, imagine teaching a person to walk by talking to them. We don't learn to walk that way, we learn to walk by falling down a lot in our attempts to get to where we imagine we want to be. At no point in the process are there lists of facts to memorize. Instead, such facts as may be needed may be derived from (because they are inherent in) physical memory. Having mastered walking correctly, running is within easy reach. Though it is nothing as simple as extending the same skill, mastery of a musical instrument makes subsequent training on other instruments much easier, even if they are not in the same family of instruments. This might suggest that the information stored in our bodies is arranged in a very sophisticated way.

Even a person who is weak, inept or impaired can acquire principles through physical training. It is a way of learning that changes one physically, both by re-organizing the musculoskeletal system and by building new neural pathways.

This has little to do with natural talent, prowess or proficiency, and everything to do with correct practice.

The art of the sword provides a direct gauge of both correct practice and progress in two ways. It invokes the urgency of life and death, focusing attention. And it is as uncaring and indifferent to the user as the stars in the night sky. Only correct application will fulfill its function. This instantly reveals every flaw in execution through clear feedback from the laws of Physics (and from the Instructor, which amounts to the same thing for practical purposes. The latter supersedes the former when in doubt).

In Zen the body and the mind are one. When I take up the sword and cut, that is all that stands in the way of perfection. Everything I think, and everything I do, is the mind. The sword, while just a sword, also accounts for the other part of the equation of Zen and the mind: *Zen ken ichi,* "Zen and the sword are one." A sword is absolutely indifferent to the mind, more indifferent if possible than the fierce old Zen master that is my instructor. Even as a representation of Zen the sword is without parallel.

"We do not bend the Art to ourselves; we bend ourselves to the Art." This bending is quite severe and rigorous. Even with the discipline applied in the dôjô there is still the past to contend with. We develop habitual ways of moving that can be very difficult to change. Think of how the people you know walk. You can probably identify them at a distance by their familiar gait.

After training for about twenty-six years this was made even more clear to me by an inflammatory infection of the peripheral nerves. The medical world is still in doubt as to the cause of this, and fortunately it was temporary, but one fine day nerve tissue began to disappear, switching off fine motor functions and skin sensations, progressing inwards from the fingers and toes. I was unable to walk within a week. There was no telling whether it would stop before my breathing shut down.

Science came to my rescue. An eminent neurologist presented my case to his students. "Test, test, test," he said to them, "All you want to do is test! But what do you expect to find?" He proceeded to make the diagnosis using only his knowledge, a safety pin, and a few simple questions. I felt like the 'Cello at a master class by Yo-Yo Ma. He then ordered two tests, predicting accurately what they would confirm, and administered therapy that pulled me back from the brink of total immobility.

As soon as I could tie my own *hakama* I staggered back into the dôjô and made a direct if not strictly scientific discovery about muscle memory. The idea of muscle memory is that somehow, muscles remember movements. Strictly speaking, muscles only contract in response to nerve impulses from the brain and/or spinal cord. But the term does convey something, and for me it conveys something quite specific since the following curious episode.

There is a certain rather beautiful and terrifying kata I had never been able to perform at all convincingly. Legend has it that this form was invented by Sasaki Kojiro, Musashi's last adversary, who was said to be able to cut birds out of the air with his sword, "Clothes-pole." It involves dropping suddenly to the ground (presumably avoiding beheading) while drawing the sword, extending it to the right, then spiraling left and upwards in one sweeping cut around to the rear, coming to a tall stance on the left leg, finally cutting down vigorously.

It can destroy even a young set of knees. In the past when I had tried this kata my legs would buckle and I would lose my balance. My performance had never been either beautiful or terrifying, and any performance that is not both beautiful and terrifying is a poor, sad thing. After my forced vacation, when my legs had regained some of their strength, I tried it. To my astonishment, everything worked the way it is supposed to work. Still no beauty or terror, but it was much improved.

The only explanation that makes sense to me is that the nerve damage erased established (but incorrect) neural pathways. Our nervous system tends to take familiar routes rather than grow new ones. It has something to do with mapping. It is good enough for most circumstances. Once mapped, these pathways are difficult to replace with better ones. This is why correct practice is so important. To get a feel for this, try writing with the wrong hand. The movements are possible, but not organized. Fine tuning would mean physically growing new neural pathways, and then creating new maps. This is quite a lot of work for a nervous system.

My recovery process involved re-growth of nerve tissue from the spinal cord to the tips of fingers and toes. The familiar mappings were still in my brain, but the roads the maps refer to had been torn up. In the case of this particular exercise, I had the data without the neural routes. Now, in the absence of even rough roads, I had to grow them.

This offers little help in correcting bad habits. Without another accident to clear the system, I would probably be hard pressed to make significant modifications. This is certainly true of basic skills like walking. It took nearly a year to regain some semblance of a normal gait. Gross movement returned first, followed oh, so slowly by finer motor control.

I now see practice as the process of making neural maps. The nerve pathways are grown to implement these, so if practice is correct, the neural pathways will grow correctly. If not, we may be stuck with something close, but wrong. The only way to fix that is extremely slow, detailed, repeated movement. Practice, as Sensei always says, makes permanent, not perfect. If you train in these arts, your body is going to hurt. It has never before done anything correctly. Until now not one muscle has ever been applied in the right way. The process of re-learning its fundamental workings seems difficult and time-consuming. This is because it is difficult and time-consuming. The urgent confrontation with one's own body – more precisely, where we confront the mind – is the point where hammer meets anvil in the forge of Budô. Putting the body through this process rearranges habits of mind as radically as those of movement, and the importance of this should not be overlooked. There is no shortcut.

In the West we learn through social pressure that failure is to be avoided at all costs. Students try to play down what they don't know. But in the dôjô we learn that failure is merely what learning feels like. Somewhere along the line we attached a word and a load of meaning to that feeling, but now it becomes a reliable and trusted friend. In the dôjô, a person who never fails is not likely to be doing much of anything worthwhile, certainly not learning.

I recall classes with our headmaster, in which my Instructor, his senior student, performed a technique over and over again like the rest of us, as if he were the newest white belt. It was astonishing to see this man, a master in his own right, stumbling and getting up and trying again, working his way through the movements our teacher had presented. He had emptied himself of everything he knew, and approached this class in total humility, trying and failing and trying again until he had it exactly right. He was smiling and cheerful, and utterly without the slightest embarrassment at being so apparently clumsy and inept. Yet I had seen this man leap into the air from *seiza*, draw and cut, returning the sword to the *saya* before landing again in seiza.

Training in Budô will make the brain hurt, too. This would follow, since it turns out we have also had little practice at using that part of the body correctly. Using the brain at all is a step forward: it may be some time before the brain stops using the student. Training in this art, though it is arduous and painful, is actually about 98 percent brain training. Said Sensei, "Treat your brain like any other muscle, work it 'til it hurts!"

This section is titled "Body." If this seems to have been stretched in some ways, it probably is because in English we learn to think of body, mind and spirit as if they were three different things. In the dôjô there is scant vocabulary for such abstractions. Yet we do train to organize all our parts so that they operate without internal conflict. A person who is fully aligned and integrated may appear incredibly strong and powerful, but this is not some mysterious energy, it is the normal high-functioning state of a human being.

Once, in a bit of inadvertent mondo, a student said to Sensei that he wanted to unify body, mind and spirit. Sensei said, "If they were not already unified, you would be dead. More practice!"

In the dôjô we only need concern ourselves with three things: keiko, keiko, keiko.

23 MIND

In his ground-breaking book, "The Way and The Power," F.J. Lovret wrote: "The essence of life is struggle and its goal is domination." It is tempting to read this as a glib explanation for our bloody history, and a justification for a grim future. But human history is not accounted for by anything so simple as Kipling's Law of the Jungle. Far from being a simplistic platitude, the statement goes much deeper.

We speak as if there were objective reality. Perhaps there is; but cling as we may to the notion that we truly see it, many ancient philosophical and religious traditions, modern brain research, and comedy, all suggest that our limited view is probably as much of it as we will ever see.

Our view of the world is just that, a view, a prospect, an image of what may possibly exist. Constructed in the brain, and bearing only a metaphorical resemblance to whatever actuality it represents, it is unique to each of us, and very much a product of our apparatus of perception.

Brains are not built to perceive the world as it is: they are only what has been successful at enhancing species survival. Direct experience could make no sense, without the interpretive and contextual processing our brains perform. We seem to take in information from our eyes, ears, nose, tongue, and skin, but the perceptions that arise are flavored and colored and modulated in a mental model of the world, sufficient to avoid danger, capture prey, find mates, and generally sustain the species. A brain is a sort of prognosticating machine for the immediate future. And that's all we've ever needed to keep our gene pool swirling, so that's what we have to work with between our ears.

Our brain-generated model of life provides all that we know about what is happening around us. Much of it is composed of language, and along with language comes the appearance of cause and effect and sequential time and Meaning. This is sufficient to anticipate situations to a certain degree of reliability. What more could one wish for? Perhaps a little more emphasis on individual survival.

Make no mistake: the goal of life's struggle is not your individual dominance, it's the dominance of your genes. You are only a pawn in that game. One of seven billion human pawns, among several trillions of other living entities. A great many of these live inside us, performing essential functions within our very cells. We are colonies of living things, cooperative and competitive, whether interdependent or inimical.

Lovret's observation eloquently describes the mind's fundamental operating principle. There is constant threat-assessment within this mental model of the world, so the model must also contain a symbol of something to protect. We know it by various names, such as "myself". It too is part of the model. Although this "myself" is a representation, whatever is deemed a threat to it is fairly likely to have a counterpart in reality that places the being in jeopardy. With the full arsenal of chemical triggers at the brain's disposal, an approximately appropriate response may be initiated before we are aware of it.

Most of the time "you" are a passenger on this ride. The mind's function is to perpetuate whatever past is represented in a story about "me", in "my" struggle for domination and survival. Statistically, this is as close to actual survival as need be, to keep humanity going. But it may be insufficient to keep you going.

It is as if the brain identifies a set of problems to represent "me" and works around the clock to maintain the status quo, which is at least not death. Could it be that those familiar, recurring difficulties are part of this virtual identity? Perhaps this is why every solution tends to multiply problems, rather than resolve them. But worse yet: maybe this constructed "me" is not merely accompanied by this set of problems: maybe the problems are *all there is of "myself"*.

Apparatus evolved for statistical success of the community suggests that "my" success is related to the success of people around me. In that case, keeping the set of community problems called "me" going is far more important to our gene pool than satisfying "my" personal wants and needs; or for that matter, keeping "me" alive at all. In which case, I will not notice or remember the difference. Whenever something happens, most of the time the explanations after the fact will satisfy "me" that it was "my" exercise of free will and intelligence that have saved the day.

Rarely, but inevitably, the fantasy world will collide with the actual. Sometimes with less than catastrophic results. This state of affairs is the basis for comedy.

Most of Charlie Chaplain's films explored this in depth. People who undergo physical training of any kind can appreciate Chaplin's uncanny athletic abilities. Making the extraordinary look easy is a mark of mastery, and this man, whose skill at movement was unparalleled, made his antics look downright accidental. Even camera tricks, such as filming backwards, required incredible skill. Charlie on the deck of a storm-tossed ship, carrying the Captain's tea service, while the deck does a three hundred sixty degree roll; he keeps the tray level regardless of what the world does. Charlie as a bricklayer, catching tossed bricks with his elbows and knees and laying them in fresh mortar, would still have to take them from the wall, balance them and drop them with total precision to achieve this startling effect when the film was reversed.

MATTERS OF LIFE AND DEATH

I recall as a youngster being allowed to attend the Chaplin Seminars put on by the head of the Astronomy Department at the college where my father taught. Professor Van De Camp, in addition to being the first to discover a planetary body outside of our solar system, possessed reels of almost everything Chaplin ever put on film. He played the piano accompaniment to these silent films (composed, I think, by the great director himself) with the broad range of emotion and color Chaplin had at his disposal before color and sound were possible in moving pictures. One always forgot that there was no color when the bashful Tramp presented The Girl with a fresh-picked flower.

In one film of my memory Charlie is idly observing the passing scene, alternately twirling his bamboo cane behind him and leaning on it, rocking back on his heels in time to some tune he is whistling – innocently unaware that his stick is landing on one of the crossbars of a storm drain as it takes his weight and springs him upright again. The audience is riveted: when will the stick go between the bars destroying this picture of suave nonchalance? When will The Little Tramp's private world converge with the real one? When it does, we laugh not at his discomfiture, but with sympathetic recognition of a rude awakening. Comedy aims to bring about such awakenings, penetrating our blindness to the life around us.

True Comedy has this in common with Zen. A *Satori* is often accompanied by laughter. This is the same helpless laughter that overtakes me whenever I am the recipient of Sensei's *Aikijutsu*. It has something to do with being face to face with undeniable reality, with no recourse to illusion. We are thrust into the present, where there is no language. But there is expression, of life.

By such fortuitous experiences we all know intuitively that there is a state of being that transcends the state of Ego, which is to say, there is a way of being not entirely devoted to perpetuating one's story about one's imagined self. This discovery must bear on our genetic success, otherwise it would probably not be possible. Glimpsing the mutability of reality, we also notice that we might not be snuffed out the second our guard is down. Life may not all be a state of constant threat. We just don't use our perceptual equipment for much else. But somehow we can be impelled to laugh. In such moments we "forget ourselves." In other words, "I" ceases to exist.

In training we find that rather than attempt to cover all possible threats with options and counter-measures, we can develop a way of being open to whatever happens, without the ceaseless assessment that removes us from present awareness. We can respond appropriately to actual conditions, rather than acting out some similar-seeming past event.

In Kenjutsu this open attitude is called *happobiraki*, "open in eight directions". It is not necessarily easy to enter this state of being just because we are told it is possible, much less to sustain it. It requires earnest study, and this is all physical training. But it is possible for anyone to develop this oddly powerful kind of vulnerability.

The discovery that the world and our view of it are not the same just might be the jewel beyond price all our ancient sages have been pointing to for thousands of years. It has the peculiar quality that it can only be discovered by your own efforts. Enlightenment can happen, but only to you, and only now!

MATTERS OF LIFE AND DEATH

24 SPIRIT

Spirit, Body and Mind may not be so distinct in Zen traditions. When Sensei mentions spirit, it is probably not your immortal soul he is talking about. He might refer to the flavor of a technique, or the feeling evoked by a performance. A kata may have specific emotional content. Since every movement is choreographed to the last detail, this must be conveyed without the normal perceptual queues. Spirit may also be involved in techniques that, correctly applied, appear magical. In addition to deceptive tactics, feints and timing designed to induce an opponent to react in predictable ways, some strategies rely on what are now known as mirror neurons, the "monkey-see, monkey-do" brain cells that may induce us to match another's actions. As an example of how this works, you might recall a singing performance that left you with a sore throat from unconsciously following the singer's vocal pyrotechnics. Budô and brain science are not far apart.

Spirit, as a term of art, extends beyond performance and neuroscience. There is a definite sensibility to a proper dôjô that seasoned practitioners will pick up immediately. It is like a resonance we feel when handling an ancient artifact. In the Shinto traditions, even rocks contain some spiritual essence, but whether some consciousness actually dwells in these spaces or objects is of little concern when we come out of such a dôjô after a particularly intense session. We pause, breathing in the essence of each feature of the landscape. We are not worried about whether there are such things as *Kami* inhabiting the rocks and trees. The experience to which this refers, like all actual experience, is entirely non-conceptual. Any way we describe it, a dôjô that lacks it is palpably impoverished.

In the traditional dôjô, A Kami is thought to inhabit the *Kamiza* ("Kami seat"), the formal focal point of the room. This is usually a tiny house on a special shelf, with doors and perhaps a little stairway in the front, but it may be almost anything, a bonsai, a stone, or an ornate Buddhist shrine. Assiduous training feeds whatever inhabits this traditional object, whereas laxity may have the opposite effect. In the context of Budô it is a useful way of looking at things. Train as hard as you can! Don't starve the Kami!

25 POWER

Ordinarily we describe power in mechanical, political, mental, spiritual and even magical terms, all having to do with results produced by a quantity of effort, whether applied or held in reserve to initiate a specific chain of cause and effect. But this utilitarian description is actually the definition of force.

Power has more to do with being at the source of life. A helpless infant is not without power. There may be results that are not adequately explained by mechanical effort.

Suppose a person without training attempts to lift an upright piano. They approach this by assuming a strong position, and if reasonably careful, they apply force with thigh and diaphragm, pushing against the floor. Since a piano is too heavy for most people to lift, they strain every muscle, exerting maximum tension. They close off the throat, using the lungs and viscera as a cushion for more leverage. The face turns red, then a blotchy purple, contorting in a terrifying grimace, teeth grinding. The piano moves, or doesn't. With a loud, explosive exhalation they drop everything.

Now a person with a few years of martial arts training arrives. They place themselves as did our muscular friend. But here they behave differently. They grasp the piano, set their posture, inhale deeply, breathe out steadily, and without facial contortions, up goes the piano. What makes the difference?

If we were to feel the muscles this person uses to lift, they would be in full tension. But unlike our untrained piano mover, the opposing muscles would be totally relaxed. Nothing not actually needed in lifting the piano would be tense. The abdomen might be solid, but the breath would not be constrained at all, the face composed.

Except for a few skilled professionals, people do not usually separate the muscle sets needed for a job from those they don't need. Instead every muscle in the area is flexed more or less indiscriminately. Then the unneeded muscles operate in opposition to the ones actually doing the work. We might put forth tremendous effort with little to show for it, and call the work difficult.

Visiting a dôjô devoted to a related art, I was invited to join a class. We were instructed to grasp our training partner by both wrists. If the grip was soft, the partner should respond with a certain throw to the rear; if the grip was hard, apply a straight-arm counter-thrust. When I took a very firm hold my partner performed as directed, thrusting straight back against my hands. Instead of being propelled backwards by my own rigid arms, my relaxed elbows bent, defeating the technique. My partner, who was familiar with this technique, looked surprised. But there was nothing wrong in his execution. His problem was my years of practice with a sword. A strong sword grip does not require tension in the upper arms: to the contrary, flexibility is critical. Although their art had historical roots in swordsmanship, they seldom practiced with the sword. In this way good technique will devolve to incomprehensible gestures and false expectations of effectiveness.

Most people never need to become organized beyond what might be called our default setting at birth. The level of organization that develops in the course of training is dramatically higher.

As the old teachings point out, strategy is independent of scale – "one man, ten thousand men" – and even conflicts between muscle sets in one's arm are similar in principle to conflicts between siblings, villages or opposing armies. Strategies embodied in physical movements apply at every level. For example, the well-known "divide and conquer" is exemplified in our first example, in opposing muscle-sets canceling each other out.

The power of an efficient, well-organized physical body is only part of the story. Human conflict takes place in and between minds. Notions about how we evolved intelligence to feed and protect ourselves in the presence of large predators would not seem sufficient to account for this unique appendage: many other creatures face the same problem without such a radical adaptation. But competition with other groups of proto-hominids is quite different. After the large predators are outwitted and eaten, new problems are certain to arise. It seems inevitable that we would reach a point beyond which even well-coordinated force alone could not decide the outcome.

Despite the apparent necessities that gave it birth, Budô is not about managing threats or making them. It's not about getting better at violence. It is absolutely not about "security", it recognizes no such thing, and urges us to abandon any such notions. Ultimately the quest for survival, and then for dominance, has lead to an awakening to something beyond the repetition of automatic survival reactions derived from past events.

In a traditional dôjô we operate in such a way as to test the limits of power beyond what is reasonable. My Instructor requires the class to walk past him without stopping or changing pace. As I pass him his arm blocks my path at chest height. He outweighs me by fifty pounds, and it's all solid muscle. I feel as if I've hit a wall.

He then works with the class to invoke a different state of mind. I relax, set my gaze far into the distance, and lower my center, something that only makes sense to say after some months of intensive training. Then I move forward, with no thought of an arm or a wall or anything in the way. Without effort, I walk on by, regardless of all opposition.

Force is inadequate to explain this: no matter how well organized I am, the opposing force is measurably overwhelming. Concretely, he is capable of stopping a much larger person than I am. But from the standpoint of power, my perception of my Instructor's strength was only an assumption on my part, which having been abandoned, no longer held me back.

However this may be, this experience forced a change in perception. Over the years there have been many demonstrations that my view of life is suspect. I know far less than I did in the beginning, which in this context does not seem like much of a loss.

26 RESISTANCE

In the exercise called *Kokyudôsa*, I sit on my heels, knee to knee with a partner. We bow to each other. My opponent grips both my wrists and attempts to hold me in place. Some schools teach that the object of this exercise is to work around the opponent's strength and execute a throw skillfully, with minimal exertion. In the traditional form one flies in the face of adversity, throwing the opponent over backwards. To do this the first thing I must overcome is an idea about what is possible. I empty my lungs, and my mind.

Resistance shapes us. We usually think of it as an opposing force. Often we oppose ourselves. This can occur physically, as when lifting a heavy weight, straining opposing muscle groups, canceling out much of our strength. It can happen with ideas.

That we are shaped by what we resist is merely a fact of structural engineering. We erect those structures that match opposing force exactly. There are always many such structures in equilibrium. Just to stand on our feet, resistance must exactly match gravity.

But also, what we resist may not exist at all. The principle still applies. We often assume the shape of something that isn't really there. Often we resist embarrassment, boredom, or even what we see as success, and walk around bored, embarrassed and unsatisfied. Some people resist what they call violence. The teaching "Resist not evil" attributed to Jesus Christ, or Lao Tse's "The superior man does not contend" make perfect sense in this light. Resist not evil, lest you assume its identical shape. "Judge not, that ye be not judged." Don't wait for your karma, it is here already.

There is a popular notion that the power of martial arts lies in using the enemy's strength against them. There are hundreds of techniques for exploiting momentum and inertia, seeking a line of least resistance. This is certainly appealing to those of us who may not be heavyweights. But we waste a tremendous amount of power against ourselves.

As I relax into emptiness my partner's grip tightens around my wrists – and around my mind. I can only guess where the opponent's strength lies based on perception, nothing more. Normally I accept such evidence as interchangeable with reality. Normally that serves well enough to get across the street safely. But the Way challenges everything and accepts no assumptions.

Resistance is relative. For practical purposes, it matters little whose resistance it is, since resistance is only to be measured between two opposing forces. If I perceive such a thing as a "line of resistance," is the opposing force just equal to my own strength, or is it the size of a mountain? Am I pushing against an equal and opposite force, or leaning against a wall of solid rock? If I push harder, does my opponent? How can I tell? Or is what I perceive my own resistance, misidentified as the opponent's?

One possibility is that what seems to be the line of most resistance is where I will find my own illusions at their most solid. If the mere perception of opposing strength forms a boundary I cannot cross, I am hemmed in on all sides by nothing but my own mind. The existence of an opponent hardly matters. That is why the Instructor says to forget all that, and just take the line of most resistance, as if to skewer myself on the enemy's blade so as to slide down it to get at them.

I expand outward oblivious to resistance, and my opponent tips over backwards.

Then we trade places.

27 REISHIKI

In Western dôjô Reishiki is often explained to new arrivals as discipline, manners or etiquette, a strict set of rules about everything, when to bow, how deeply and to whom, where to sit, when you may eat, and so on. There is nothing peculiar to martial arts in this; it is what Japanese children learn before they enter school.

F. J. Lovret has written that Japanese training is a form of applied Behaviorism. I had strong opinions about the field in which this is a term-of-art, which led me to do some research.

Behaviorism is a set of psychological theories proposing that behavior is the result of external stimuli, and can be modified through application of the right ones. Since its formulation by B. F. Skinner, who mostly confined his experimental work to laboratory rats and pigeons, it has found its way into politics, education, law enforcement, religion and economic policy, for a few examples. The background assumption is that people must be subjected to the right rewards and punishments, or they will behave badly. Possibly in these instances this is not a new system, but merely a new set of labels on a very old form of government. In Academia, at least, there is an opposing view that takes into account the fact that people also can be creative and think for themselves. After fifty years, controversy still rages among the Behaviorists and the Mentalists as to the roots of human behavior. World wars have been fought over questions of practical application.

More recently, exploring and mapping the dim reaches of the human brain, researchers have found indications of a strong and predictable connection between the ways we behave, and the way life appears to us in a given moment or situation. While the Behaviorists seemed to discount perception as a factor, behavior is now widely seen to be consistent with perception, and only coincidentally with specific outside stimuli. So it would seem prohibitively complex to attempt to create the right stimuli to produce a desired set of behaviors in human beings, the way Skinner tried to do with laboratory rats and pigeons.

Perception is the product of processing sensory input, which is directly measurable in the brain with modern equipment. Perception is not the same as the actual world, being at best a rather crude representation of it. As an ancient Zen master put it, "You do not see when seeing; you do not hear when hearing." And that too has by now been directly verified through rigorous scientific research. Much of what we "see" and "hear" is composed of previous visual and aural images. We respond to life as we experience it through our brains, not as it is. Perception is what tunes our attitudes, thinking, physical experience and emotions, shaping conduct and demeanor. It is not our actual situation that drives the way we act; it is what we believe about our situation that drives the way we act.

Not only do we not see or hear, we do not even make decisions. For example, deciding to swing at a baseball takes more processing time in a batter's brain than a ball takes to get from the pitcher's hand to Home Base. That decision to swing is all settled before the pitcher begins the windup, before the batter thinks of whether to swing: the experience of deciding to swing is a sort of instant replay. The batter believes it is a real decision, but it is actually a pre-set pattern of neurons firing.

The adaptive purpose of this little simulation could well be to keep us from actually doing anything ourselves, since for the most part our brains are much better at handling our affairs without our help. From the standpoint of species survival this has been working fairly well. Some years ago a popular joke had it that in future computer installations there would be a man and a dog: the man there to feed the dog, and the dog there to keep the man from touching the computer. It is not a bad analogy. Our individual flashes of brilliance could well impair our statistical success as a species. So far, so good, at least. This too could change, now that we are figuring out how our brains actually work.

Baseball, incidentally, is one of the applications to which the Japanese have brought their training methods with considerable effectiveness, so perhaps all is not lost.

Let us look again at what brain science is telling us. Some of us may be in for a bit of a shock. Here is what we now know – that is, what Scientists say they have not been able to falsify, which is as close to saying something is true as any Scientist should ever be willing to get:

1. You don't decide anything when you think you are deciding; that is just a mental picture of you making a decision that has already been made.

2. You don't see what you think you are seeing. Only a very small part of the retinal image comes through the lens of the eye; this gets fitted into a brain-generated picture composed of previous images, on the rest of the retina, before the visual image is processed for you to "see." This system allows us to keep up with events better than if we had to process each detail, each moment.

3. It is probably just as well; there is no you in there anyway. "You" are just more neuronal patterns in the brain.

In the face of all this we may well ask, what is going on in the dôjô? And where does Reishiki come in?

Outward expression is connected in some close way with perception. And perception is malleable. This is the role of discipline, to refract and bend and modify, perhaps refine, perception. If we ourselves create a kind of perceptual lens through which to approach life, rather than an external, arbitrary set of prods and promptings, a form of applied behaviorism is an apt description. The followers of both Professors Skinner and Chomsky (who roundly refuted Skinner in a famous book review) might object to the nomenclature, because we are in effect filtering external stimuli, which the Skinnereans would deny, and the Chomskyites call a misnomer. Regardless, Reishiki, as with mathematics or medicine or military science, harnesses the brain to generate performance consistent with the world as perceived through its specialized lens.

This is entirely separate from the techniques and principles that distinguish a particular art. There is a level of mastery accessible through Reishiki without regard to which school of which art one pursues.

There is Reishiki for every moment. I enter the dôjô in special clothing, moving with quiet formality, fixing my gaze in a special way, paying my respects to the ryû, the Instructor, my fellow deshi. Then, zazen. This is another world. We perform with ritual precision, matching our breathing, responding in the same moment. My attention is outwards, awareness reaching beyond the walls. My thoughts have faded to nothing, and with them, "me." All that remains is performance. What happens, happens without evaluation or preference or memory. In "my" absence, there is still a presence-of-mind (for want of a better term). Perhaps it is what we call *Zanshin*.

Reishiki is a bit more powerful than a list of Dôjô Do's and Don't's. In Reishiki, it doesn't really matter if there is no you in there. The brain will go on generating that convenient fiction, and like our Baseball player's brain, it will go on swinging at the ball, and providing the representation of you with a representation of the decision to swing at a representation of a ball.

We have but to interpose a certain discipline at the perceptual end, to link up our momentary responses. In this sense we may say it is a way of shaping behavior. However, we are creating, not a stimulus-response machine, but a context, a world, within which action is consistent with Budô: Reishiki and the Way are one.

Sensei was right, of course. And more than a few steps ahead of Western Science.

MATTERS OF LIFE AND DEATH

28 DEATH

Death is not something we can remember and anticipate, since we have never died. Objectively, death comes only once. Subjectively, which is our only mode of experience, it never does.

The Samurai attitude towards death is perhaps their defining characteristic in the West. If they find their way into the literature, most martial arts students encounter something about choosing death over life. This does not make sense right away, if ever. As a white belt my first reaction – actually I don't remember it. This shows how much of a cultural frame of reference exists for the idea, where I was born and brought up: none whatsoever. "When you leave the eaves of your house, you are already a dead man." What did that mean? I had no idea. I wanted to stay alive! I thought that was the whole point of training.

There is nothing quite so elusive as the idea of my own death. There have been times when this idea was very detailed, and accompanied by a sudden and compelling physical response. There have been events in which certain death passed very close by, but it did not register. I reacted automatically, involuntarily, and often, inappropriately. In each case, thought came much too late to be useful. I have to conclude that thinking is not going to happen at the moment of death. It probably isn't going to hurt.

I once found a baby raccoon in the snow, half its face bristling with porcupine quills. It would die unless they were removed. I had extracted quills from dogs; what did I have to fear from this cute little ball of fluff? Seeing myself as a compassionate being, I decided to capture the tiny creature. I managed to corner it, and moved in – and it launched itself at me with teeth bared, hissing loudly, every hair standing on end! I lost all sense of proportion. My skin seemed to shrink all at once, and before I knew it I had retreated a good ten feet, heart pounding, gasping for breath. My physical reaction would have been more appropriate had it been a charging bear, although we are advised, here in bear country, to stand our ground when it comes to charging bears. I doubt whether I will have any say in the matter. My endocrine system will probably take over.

On another occasion my mid-brain triggered the "fight" response. I was not expecting a fight; I wasn't even in a bad neighborhood. I was at work outdoors when a rifle bullet buried itself in a piece of timber near my head. Then I heard shots. When I understood what this was – but not what it meant, apparently – I flew into a rage and ran in the direction of the shooter, shouting something about his ancestry, never thinking about taking cover. I was sure I could see the tracks of the bullets cutting through the tall grasses, inches to the right and left. I had no sense of danger. When the man saw me running toward him, he dropped the weapon and threw his hands up. He had been adjusting the sights on his deer rifle.

This was not bravery, any more than my retreat from a baby animal was cowardice. The lizard-brain reacts instantly. Other parts of the brain explain what happened later, most likely inventing a heroic story. A charging baby raccoon got the flight response and I back-pedaled before I knew it. Flying bullets elicited the opposite response, and I charged just as thoughtlessly.

What is "threat", and what is "self"? Seeing the world through a mental representation of reality, must not the "self" also be symbolically represented, for the model to function at all? The self we protect may be no more than a symbol in a dream. It may trigger appropriate responses to actual events, or may not. But there is no model of death in there. There is no need for it. No response will be necessary if it happens, and none will be possible.

To respond to real life in real time is only necessary, from a biological standpoint, to the degree that enough individuals survive more often than not. But there is no need to experience actual, present reality for that to work. A primitive reaction may serve the purpose regardless of one's experience. To be more finely attuned to present reality is possible, but not statistically necessary as far as the species is concerned. Full awareness in the moment is optional. If my imaginary escape from imaginary danger stimulates my real body to appropriate action well enough, often enough, what does it matter that I experience all this in a heroic fantasy? We accumulate experiences that might be useful in a range of possible events, but we cannot recall and anticipate every possible eventuality. We collect memories representing survival. For enough of us, enough of the time, these representations triggered by similarity to present events have been sufficient.

This is all well and good, until we stand at swords' points. In that case, relying on the hormones released by glands triggered by symbolic threats to a symbolic "self" within a mental map of the world, has some obvious limitations. Events often move faster than the brain's processing capacity, even with all the shortcuts it deploys to keep up. Even if it were quick enough, such a system can also be fooled.

One's own survival mechanisms can be taken over by the enemy, using strategy and tactics that simply avoid triggering the system, or trigger some inappropriate response.

On the other hand, with proper training, a person responding to actual events in the present moment, and not immersed in memory, may possibly respond instantly to an opponent's intentions before any action occurs. This is described in ancient texts in great detail, but may not be recognized if the reader has no experiential reference.

Whether danger is real or imagined, it is all the same to the endocrine system that controls most of our responses. Books of divination may work perfectly, but only after the fact do we slap the forehead and exclaim, "Oh! That's what 'cross the great river' meant!" To arrive at a reality represented by a concept is not a trivial matter, since the concept is from the past. I know a baby raccoon cannot do much damage unless it has rabies; I know a rifle bullet can kill me instantly. None of this conceptual knowledge affected my behavior. It simply wasn't available until the action was over.

All of this implies, not that our survival systems are flawed, but that there might be a way of knowing the world of present reality, other than the manipulation of symbols in a representational model in my head. If ordinary thought processes are confined to the application of programmed responses from remembered events, this is unlikely to supersede reactions triggered in the mid-brain. If reacting is too crude, and thinking is constrained to the past, could there be some third way in our human being that can be brought to bear?

Whatever this third way might be, some faculty or sensory organ, or some new way of seeing through the senses we know about, it appears that we have little or no access to it through thinking, except perhaps in the way that physicists predict the existence of particles too small to observe directly.

The mind is devoted to avoiding danger. In avoiding danger, I also avoid the present. Everything is seen through the lens of memory. Could it be that I equate presence with death? Like my death, the present moment is not something I can remember and anticipate. The present moment is unknown and unknowable territory. In the present moment I have no idea what do to, in fact I have no ideas at all, yet. Nothing has happened, as far as "I" am concerned.

Before I leave my house, I am present. Is this not the same as saying I am already a dead man? In "choosing death" I choose to be present in this, possibly my last moment of life. It sounds simple enough.

MATTERS OF LIFE AND DEATH

29 VOID

Throughout the literature of Zen and the Japanese arts we encounter this strange idea of Void. Like the Arab invention, zero, it is not simply nothingness. Absolutely unlike that stroke of mathematical genius it is not at all conceptual. Everything we can imagine comes from something else that already exists. Anything wholly new seems beyond imagining. The same holds true for action: try moving without thinking first. If you succeeded, what a surprise!

Faced with an adversary's sword, true spontaneity is a matter of life and death. Originating anything is impossible through changing what is already present. Creation can be available only beyond the realm of what we know. Original thought and action comes from a kind of no-where, an emptiness, but a necessary emptiness for anything created. We call this the Void.

Bearing in mind that we are in the realm of language, we may describe this Void by inference. In the moment, original action is a direct expression of the being, without passing through a sequence of cognitive functions.

This can be seen when senior swordsmen square off. The attack and response are simultaneous, "without space for a hair to pass between them." It may seem as if the opponents both decide to begin independently, at the same instant, but is not the same thing as synchronizing with another person. Neither is it a lucky guess.

There are two reliable methods for acquiring this skill, if we may speak of it that way: Zazen, or Zen sitting, and keiko, repetitive and relentless training. In both disciplines there is an objective measure against which we may discern the mind at work. In zazen the typical instruction is to sit, and only sit; do not think about not thinking; just, sit. Very soon it will become quite obvious that much other than just sitting is going on. With the sword, just cut. It is almost impossible to reduce the performance to no more than what is necessary, and the perfect cut is thrown off to the degree that we bring anything extraneous to the task. That degree delineates the boundaries of the mind, or the edges of Void.

30 HARAGEI

Among the unique faculties cultivated in sword training is *Haragei*, a word with no standard English counterpart. "Gut feeling" does not quite convey the sense of it. *Haragei* is not exactly awareness of one's surroundings, and not hyper-vigilance.

When I was a house carpenter, on a typical construction site there would be a motley crew of prison inmates on work-release, day-laborers, and journeymen with their own tools. On one such job, among this group of professionals there was a man with a twisted sense of humor who liked to tease those he considered inferior to himself. On an especially cold winter day, when snow made work more dangerous and uncomfortable than usual, and the men stood around blowing into their hands and hoping to be sent home, he staged one of his little jokes.

He summoned a slight brown man with a lost, vacant expression. "Bet you a five you can't bend this nail straight with your pinky." He hooked his little finger around one of two bent nails driven into a post, and pulled. Unbeknownst to the other man, he had previously heated the second bent nail until it almost glowed.

The intended victim did not burn his finger in this pleasant game. He smiled, and turned away. It was not the heat of the prepared nail that he sensed, but something else. Maybe it was something in the air between them.

This was too much for the prankster. For the rest of the morning he picked on the little brown man, disdainfully assigning him increasingly difficult and dirty jobs. But he never managed to elicit any response other than alacrity and good work.

We finished building the walls. The roof would be supported by large and ungainly triangular structures about thirty feet long, weighing hundreds of pounds. To get these trusses standing upright on the walls we would hang them upside-down, with the ends on the walls, and the peak toward the floor. Then several men would roll each one upright, pushing with long poles, while a man on top would fasten them in position.

We readied a batch of half a dozen trusses and began to roll them into place. It took at least four men to push one into position, and then they stood around waiting while it was secured. The crew was getting cold and hungry. As the last of the batch was pushed up they milled around waiting to see if the foreman would order another batch to be set on the walls, or tell them to knock off for lunch.

Suddenly there was a shout from above, and we looked up. The last truss had gotten loose and was beginning to tip over. It would sweep into the whole crew. It might kill people, and would certainly break bones. There was no time to think: everyone froze in place as it gathered speed.

Everyone that is, except a slight brown man, standing in the middle of the floor holding a two-by-four in one hand. He did not look up. Calmly, almost slowly, he placed that piece of wood upright in the middle of the floor with a thump. The truss came crashing down with a terrific impact that shook the building.

When we opened our eyes – nothing had happened. Hundreds of pounds of lumber had come to rest above us, in a horizontal position, the ends still on the walls, and the peak exactly on the end of that two-by-four. The little brown man stood there, still holding it, with a slight smile on his placid face. He probably saved at least one life, and several bad injuries, and he looked for all the world as if he was half asleep.

There were no more pranks.

31 SELF

What is your self?

The brain records everything that happens over our lifetime. It accesses this information according to what seems to be happening, invoking a record of a past event that is similar in some way to the present situation, providing a reaction somewhat likely to be appropriate. Even the image on the retina of your eye is mostly generated from the past, and fed back into the visual centers with the small amount of new visual information that actually arrives through the lens. Thoughts, attitudes, body sensations and emotions, combined with impressions of how the circumstances seem to be, and even how the ego appears to itself, against a background of fundamental assumptions about reality, form the perceptions that shape our behavior. Our brains also provide a "self" and a continuous narrative explaining and justifying everything the "self" does, and everything that happens to "me." We have perception, and we have a perceiver. This is sufficient to account for the entire drama of a life. This is all well known to brain scientists. What is not known, is where, in all this lifeless, mechanical, automatic survival machinery, the self can be found.

Occasionally a situation arises that this clockwork ego cannot cope with. Ordinarily it covers this by ignoring the gaps in the fundamental assumptions that form the context of "my" experience, going on as if nothing were amiss. The alternative, so far as ego is concerned, is death. Consider that the whole purpose of the ego is to perpetuate itself. Any threat to ego-survival is seen as the end of life, and most of the time the response will seem to avert disaster.

A Samurai asked a Zen monk if there really were a Hell, as described in scriptures. The monk asked what business a Samurai had inquiring into such things. The Samurai became annoyed. The monk asked if this did not amount to stealing his annual salary from his Daimyo. The Samurai, angry, put his hand on his sword. The monk said, "Now you are in Hell. Do you see?"

In the dôjô, everything is a confrontation with death. It doesn't matter whether it is physical mortality – the real possibility of severed limbs and broken bones or a fatal knock on the head – or ego-death, as this is all the same to Ego. Death is death, until it isn't. At every turn, our Sensei is killing egos like flies; some go quietly, others with histrionics worthy of the Shakespearean stage. They may not stay dead. So desperate are we to "survive," to sustain the illusion of "me," that occasionally the mind is exposed, frantically shouting "Pay no attention to that man behind the curtain!"

32 THE END / THE BEGINNING

What is the point, then, of a lifetime of strenuous training with obsolete antique weapons, or long hours spent "just sitting"?

Most of us might as well be asleep as we stumble through the only moment we have, reacting to stimuli more or less as intelligently as a box of rocks. We are individually set up to avoid death or embarrassment with about equal fervor.

But whom are we talking about? No more than patterns of electrical impulses. One, zero. On, off. A mere algorithm is living our lives. A short list of conditional instructions. If, Then, Else. That is what shapes our perceived world, and our reactions, and our sufferings.

There is no way out.

The question remains.

MATTERS OF LIFE AND DEATH

33 AXIOMS AND APHORISMS

"A Swordsman is more than just a man with a sword." [F. J. Lovret]

"The more alive you are, the harder it is to kill you." [F. J. Lovret]

"Practice does NOT make perfect; practice makes permanent." [F. J. Lovret]

"Flying through the air upside-down puts everything in perspective." [F. J. Lovret]

"Start every solo with the loudest rimshot you got." [Regi Brisbane]

"There is no way to peace. Peace IS the way." [A. J. Muste]

"Experience is a terrible teacher; it always creeps up from the inexperienced side." [Mark Twain]

"There is no reality; just your order, imposed on everything." [Frank Herbert]

"In life, understanding is the booby prize." [Werner Erhard]

"Perfection is that state in which things are the way they are, and are not the way they are not. As you can see, the universe is perfect. Don't lie about it!" [Werner Erhard]

"Invention is the mother of Necessity: when something becomes possible, it becomes necessary." [author]

"Technique is what we use after we've blown the beginning." [F. J. Lovret]

"People say, 'Man is the creature that thinks.' But I say man is the creature that counts. And he can only count to three." [F. J. Lovret]

"The *deshi* of a *ryû* as well as its instructor(s) are bound together by acts that create obligation and duty. When practiced over time in the fire of the dôjô, brotherhood and joy rise up like steam from a freshly quenched piece of iron." [J. T. Simms]

"It has been said that the unexamined life is not worth living; I say, the un-lived life is not worth examining." [Werner Erhard]

"The world is a miracle, unfolding in the pitch black." (from "The Mappist" by Barry Lopez)

"A boat builder only moves fast on two occasions; when he's making a mistake, and when he's covering it up." [old shipyard adage]

"Obsolete power corrupts obsoletely." [Theodore Holm Nelson]

"He not busy being born is busy dying." [Bob Dylan]

"A Gentleman never insults anyone unintentionally." [the author's father, Professor Carl Barus, quoting his father, quoting his]

34 HAIKU

The peculiarly Japanese form of poetry known as Haiku is familiar to Western school children. That it contains seventeen syllables is about as much as they are ever taught of the rules for the form, but there is a little more, something about the number of syllables in each line – five, seven, five, for example – and it was traditional to convey the season of the year and the weather, along with the profound poetic sensibility for which the form is justifiably famous. Poetry, calligraphy and other arts are essential to the way of swordsmanship.

A spider's web
Outside my bathroom window
Captures but windblown drops.

MATTERS OF LIFE AND DEATH

35 GLOSSARY
Common Definitions (from Merriam-Webster):

vi·o·lence
noun
Date: 14th century
1 a: exertion of physical force so as to injure or abuse (as in warfare or effecting illegal entry into a house) b: an instance of violent treatment or procedure.
2: injury by or as if by distortion, infringement, or profanation: outrage
3 a: intense, turbulent, or furious and often destructive action or force <the violence of the storm> b: vehement feeling or expression: fervor; also: an instance of such action or feeling c: a clashing or jarring quality: discordance
4: undue alteration (as of wording or sense in editing a text)
vi·o·lent
adjective
Etymology: Middle English, from Anglo-French, from Latin violentus; akin to Latin vis strength
14th century

1: marked by extreme force or sudden intense activity <a violent attack>
2 a: notably furious or vehement <a violent denunciation> b: extreme, intense <violent pain> <violent colors>
3: caused by force: not natural <a violent death>
4 a: emotionally agitated to the point of loss of self-control <became violent after an insult> b: prone to commit acts of violence <violent prison inmates>
vi·o·late
transitive verb

Etymology: Middle English, from Latin violatus, past participle of violare, from viol- (as in violentus violent)
15th century
1: break, disregard <violate the law>
2: to do harm to the person or especially the chastity of; specifically: rape
3: to fail to show proper respect for: profane <violate a shrine>
4: interrupt, disturb

Except for those in common usage in English, and proper names, common Japanese terms used in the text are italicized when they first appear. N.B.: these are not necessarily the accepted definitions of these terms, but reflect the author's own view.

Aiki, kiai: Terms related to human energy and power. In American schools some claim they mean, respectively, "coming together in harmony" and "a loud shout at the moment of striking."
The meanings in use in my experience are, respectively, "organized vital energy" and "focused power."
"Aiki" combined with *"jutsu"* or *"dô"* refers to particular grappling arts derived from swordsmanship, often but not exclusively from the Takeda family of ancient Japan. These are delineated by their *ryû* as in, *Yamate-ryû Aikijutsu, or "the aikijutsu of the Yamate-ryû"*
"Aikidô" has become the trade name of a popular practice invented by Ueshiba Morihei, a derivative of some of the Takeda teachings.

Budô: The Way (of engagement). Please see the essay, "Defining Terms."

Dô: Way, road, path. Similar to Chinese *tao.*

Dôjô: "Way place," training facility.

Hakama: Full, pleated trousers that are the traditional uniform in Japanese martial arts and in formal traditional dress.

Kami: (from Shinto religion) Spirit or entity inhabiting all sentient and non-sentient beings.

Kata: Form, prescribed series of movements to be performed exactly according to *seitei (q.v. below).* Sometimes called "*seiteigata*"). A strictly choreographed set-piece.

ki: "life-force." The difference between a living person and a corpse.

Keiko: Practice; training.

Kenjutsu: "Art of the sword," swordsmanship. (*Kendô* is "the Way of the sword." However, this, like *Aikido,* has become the generic name of a certain popular athletic form.)

Kokyu: Breath.

Kokyudôsa: A particular exercise found in most *Aikijutsu* traditions, practiced facing a partner seated knee-to-knee.

Kumitachi: A *Kata* involving two or more participants.

Makimono: Hand-wrtten scroll containing techniques or other teachings.

Mondo: In Zen, the verbal equivalent of sparring and the subject of many ancient texts recounting famous encounters between Zen masters.

Mudansha: Persons without rank in a particular discipline.

Reishiki: "Right conduct." (Please see the eponymous essay for more on this).

Ryû: The kanji has several names and several meanings, most denoting flow, tradition, continuity. In this context it refers to tradition in the sense of "The Harvard Tradition" or "The Protestant Tradition." There is the sense that a tradition is a great, deep river as old as time. Like a river, an old *ryû* will have branches and tributaries.

Seitei: The correct form, procedure or principle. Techniques may be studied in several modalities that are not *seitei,* in the process of mastering a *seitei* form, such as *bunkai* and *renshu.*

Seiza: Sitting, as people do in Japan, on the knees, between the ankles, with the great toes crossed underneath the body. This is not usually easy for people who are not used to it; however, since the first five years of sword training typically involve getting around the tatami on one's knees, or in very low stances, it is very good practice. It also tends to develop strong posture and breathing habits.

Shinza: A small shrine-like object that serves as the focus of a training area.

Tatami: The mats used in the *dojô,* usually textured vinyl reminiscent of the traditional rice-straw floor mats once used in most Japanese buildings. They are about an inch by six feet by three feet, and rooms are measured in mats, e.g., a four-mat room. *Dojô* space is often assigned to students by the number of mats they may occupy. Many old sword schools, however, have polished wood floors.

Tokonoma: An alcove in a Dôjô where certain decorative objects are displayed, also the location of the Shinza.

Yûdansha: Persons holding rank in a particular art.

Zazen: The Zen traditional practice of sitting on one's knees in a very upright posture, performing certain breathing techniques, the general purpose of which is to quiet the body and mind.

In the Way of swordsmanship this is part of training, and every session begins and ends with at least a few minutes of *zazen*. Occasionally this comprises the entire session, which may last hours or days.

Zanshin: literally, "remaining spirit." There is nothing comparable in English. It is the state of a swordsman's being.

ABOUT THE AUTHOR

Mr. Barus has trained in Kenjutsu since 1984. He holds a Senior Instructor's license and conducts regular classes, and the occasional seminar, in Kenjutsu. He lives in Vermont with his wife Lisë and assorted animals, drives a school bus, volunteers in the local community and keeps bees. He may be reached through http://barus.com.

Cover design: Christopher Hattoon
Cover art: Jerry Ostrowski
Cover photo taken at The Tômôn

Made in the USA
Lexington, KY
29 June 2014